Tales of Old Staffordshire

Other counties in this series include:

Avon
Bedfordshire
Berkshire
Buckinghamshire
Cambridgeshire
Cornwall
Devon
Dorset
East Anglia
Essex
Gloucestershire
Hampshire
Herefordshire
Hertfordshire
Kent
Leicestershire

Lincolnshire
Norfolk
Northamptonshire
Nottinghamshire
Oxfordshire
Shropshire
Somerset
Stratford
Suffolk
Surrey
Sussex
Warwickshire
Wiltshire
Worcestershire
West Yorkshire

Tales of Old Staffordshire

Kathleen Lawrence-Smith

With Illustrations by Don Osmond

COUNTRYSIDE BOOKS
NEWBURY, BERKSHIRE

First published 1992
© Kathleen Lawrence-Smith 1992

COUNTRYSIDE BOOKS
3 CATHERINE ROAD
NEWBURY, BERKSHIRE

ISBN 1 85306 207 3

Produced through MRM Associates Ltd., Reading
Typeset by Paragon Typesetters, Sandycroft, Chester
Printed in England by J W Arrowsmith Ltd., Bristol

*To my husband, Ray, who was himself a
Black Country man until responding to the
Call of King and Country!*

Acknowledgements

I am indebted to the well known writer, broadcaster and TV
personality, Phil Drabble, for his friendly and encouraging
response to my request for permission to quote from his book
Staffordshire which was published by Robert Hale in their County
series. I have retold an entertaining tale from his chapter on
Black Country Sports.

I express thanks also to the Rev. Richard Ward, retired Vicar
of The Church of the Holy Angels at Hoar Cross who supplied
me with the Centenary Celebrations brochure of that church.
I much appreciate his additional information about the Meynell
family and his trouble in helping me seek for birth dates which
do not appear on certain memorials – an omission which he
laconically describes as 'a curious shyness'.

I acknowledge also my debt to Michael Joseph Ltd.,
publishers in 1985 of *Royal Feud* by Michael Thornton, for
permission to repeat the words of Lady Rosemary Leveson-
Gower to Lady Victor Paget.

My sincere appreciation is due to Tom Byrne, author of *Tales
from the Past, Anecdotes and Incidents of North Staffordshire History*
(pubished by Remploy, 1981) for a delightful discussion and
his permission to quote from his story of Sauntering Ned in
my tale, 'Foiled by a Donkey'.

Contents

CONTENTS

STAFFORDSHIRE – The map overleaf is by John Speede, and shows the county as it was in the early 17th century.

STAFFORD

PART OF

CHES

Congleton

DYREHILL
HUNDRED

SHIRE

Draiton

Part

of

Newport

Newcastle

Stone

Stafford

CANK WOO

CUDLESTON HU

Shrop

Breewood

Newport

Shifnall

SEISDON

Wolverhampton

HUNDRED

shire

Bridgnorth

Morse Forest

Sturbridge

PART OF S
SHIR
Half-town

PART OF
FORD SHIRE

Kidderminster   PART OF

Upon Blore heath in this Countie of
Stafford, a great and bloody battayle
was fought by Richard Earle of Salesbury in the quarell of Yorke, agt
Iames Lorde Audley made Generall
for King Henry the first, wherein
the sayd Lorde Iames was slayne,
with many of the Gentillitye of Cheshire, whoe in great favour had received the yonge Prince Livery of
Swanes, and in his right manfully
fought, and lost their lives: To wit
Sir Hugh Venables, Sir Thomas Dutn
Sir Richard Molineux, Sir William
Trowtbek, Sir Iohn Leigh, Sir Iohn Dun
and Sir Iohn Edgerton Knights, & of
ye comen souldiers there dyed 2400.
men. And therein ye two sonnes of the
E. of Salesbury were taken prisoners &
sent to Chester, whence shortly they were
releasd. This battayl was fought ye 23.
day of Sept. in yere 1459. and 5 38.
of K.H.6.
raigne.

STAFFORD
COUNTIE AND TOWNE
with the ancient Citie LICHFEILD
described

SCALE OF MILES

Performed by
on Deep
Humbl. C.

LICHFIELD

Places in the Citie Lichfield
by figures obserued:

1 Stowe Church
2 Stowe Hill
3 Stowe Sever
4 Leyka lane
5 St. Michaels chur.
6 Bacon Rowe
7 Tamworth stret
8 The Chappell
9 The Conduit
10 Dams strret
11 St Chds ming.
12 Leyes lane
13 Bacon stret.
14 The Boughmast
15 Sandford stret
16 Sadlers stret
17 Bore stret

18 Wade stret
19 Tauril Hall
20 Frogg lane
21 St Iohns stret
22 St Iohns Hospitall
23 The Priory
24 The Conduit
25 The Freeschole
26 Grey Fryer lane
27 Greenhill stret
28 Bakers lane
29 Fryers lane
30 High Crosse
31 Stone Crosse
32 Damm Mill
33 Stowe Mere
34 Damm Mere

MONSLOW HUNDRED

PART OF DARBY SHIRE

PART OF LEICEST. SHIRE

PART OF WARWICK SHIRE

EAST

SOUTH

This Baronye of Stafford is very anciet
and hath bene an Earldom, the Nobles
whereof hath borne the title of Dukes
of Buckingham.

Treasure Trove in the Dove

WHAT an exciting day was the first of June, 1831! It began with a routine clearance on the banks of the river Dove to generate increased power to the cotton mills at Tutbury and speed up production. It became necessary to clear the mill race and probe for blockages in the shape of dead sheep carcases. This was a fast flowing river and many a poor creature lost balance and tumbled into the water to be submerged in gravel and silt below the surface. Then suddenly came a whoop of surprise from a workman probing 18 inches into the gravel bed. Silver coins were floating up! They were swiftly grabbed by the lucky nearest. Others rapidly abandoned tasks and rushed to the spot as hundreds more coins rose to the surface through the channel miraculously opened up by the probing rod. In no time the news spread and local worthies mustered in eager groups to get a share of the spoil. Coins were swung on to the bank by the spadeful! Never before – and never since – has there been such a day at Tutbury.

Some lucky fellows made a quick turnover, selling coins, 100 at a time, for six shillings. As demand increased the price went up to eight shillings and sixpence. 'Silver fever' struck the excited citizens. Tempers flared and fights broke out as latecomers failed to elbow their way to the front in time.

But the free for all had to end some time. When the authorities awoke to the situation, the Staffordshire Yeomanry swept in to restore order – but not before an incredible 100,000

11

silver coins had been gloatingly counted. They dated back through three reigns to the Middle Ages – and the Duchy of Lancaster came up with a dramatic claim. For their family a 500 year old mystery was solved and a tragic story given its sequel.

Their ancestor, Thomas, Earl of Lancaster was first cousin to King Edward II, and would have been a far more suitable heir to the throne. But the law of primogeniture had put the crown on Edward's unworthy head and for years cousin Thomas, whose home was Tutbury Castle, held the reins of government while the monarch played around with grasping foreign favourites. This infuriated the English nobles who fought his battles and carried his responsibilities. Thomas of Lancaster's growing opposition went unrecognised until the famous day in 1312 when the king's arrogant favourite, Piers Gaveston, was brought to book and executed.

Surely now the king would see his folly and reform? But Edward II watched and brooded, knowing his cousin Thomas had been behind Gaveston's fate – and simply repeated his folly by bringing in more foreign favourites on whom to lavish English hospitality and riches. The English nobles, led by the Earl of Lancaster and his chief ally the Earl of Hereford resolved that Edward II must be brought down.

Suddenly the king moved with unaccustomed decision, raised a force in Coventry while ostensibly there on a visit, and marched into Staffordshire to rout the rebels, primarily to avenge himself on his cousin.

The two earls were unprepared. Thomas of Lancaster hastily gathered a great store of treasure from Tutbury Castle to take to a stronghold at Pontefract, fleeing across the river Dove. The current was strong, the wagon horses stumbled, and the treasure plunged into the river! The two earls fled empty handed, pursued by the king's party and within a few days were defeated by the vengeful king in battle at Boroughbridge. The Earl of Hereford was slain and Thomas of Lancaster captured and executed on the king's orders. A ghastly day for the royal House of Lancaster.

Momentarily the despised king had triumphed, but six years later a successful revolt swept him from his throne to a death in Berkeley Castle more pitiful, more dishonourable than that of his cousin Thomas. The Earl of Lancaster was posthumously avenged.

As for the treasure, despite attempts made on behalf of the crown to dredge the river and claim the forfeiture, it was never handed over. Accusations were made that clandestine dredging had taken place and the treasure stolen away by local personalities. Some suspects were charged, but no evidence was forthcoming as to whether they had been successful in the search. So the fate of the earl's treasure remained a mystery for 500 years – until that happy summer day when fortune smiled upon the mill workers on the banks of the river Dove.

Sports and Pastimes

IN years gone by children's games had to be simple, there being no money, and nothing approaching the sophisticated gear available today. The well known game of rounders, for instance, needed no outlay beyond a cheap ball and small bat (which could be improvised if necessary) and could include almost any number of players in field or playground, divided into two teams. It was probably popular all over England, but Staffordshire added a little spice to the game by allowing the batting side's 'last man in' to make one mighty effort to reinstate all his team mates who had been caught or run out. He had to toss the ball into the air, take a great swipe at it and run *twice* around the marked stations to get 'home' before the fielding side retrieved the ball and struck him. If he succeeded, his team started their innings all over again!

Tutball was a simpler version of the same game, so called because markers indicating 'safe' stages for a player to halt if he could not run the full round, were known as 'tuts'. For tutball a bat was not required; a hand sufficed to strike the ball which was tossed by a bowler from the rival side.

Another energetic game – and a very old one – was prisoner's bars, popular here as in neighbouring Shropshire with older youths as well as children. Two teams would establish themselves in dens, clearly marked to separate them from each other. They faced a stake or boulder planted on a boundary post at least 20 yards away and equidistant from both sides. A coin having been spun, the leading man of the toss-winning side sped off to reach the stake, touch it and get back 'home' before being caught by a chaser from the opposing team. If caught he was imprisoned in their den. Even while these two ran, a second pair joined the chase, and so on. Presumably the loser of each pair – either runner or chaser – ended in the prison base, and the game ended when all or most of one side were captured. A countdown at any given time could reveal the winning team, or it could go on until only the den-keeper remained on one side. He had then to run to the boundary, and his den could be captured to cries of 'Burn the den! Burn the den!' while he was en route.

The game became so popular that in 1755 adult teams from Staffordshire and Cheshire staged a contest as a holiday attraction and wagers were laid on the result. More scandalous still in the eyes of one reporter was that the men were very scantily clothed for the occasion, 'exhibiting a Sight very improper for the Entertainment of the young Imaginations . . .' and the writer tut-tutted at the impropriety of allowing families to attend and see their fathers' undignified behaviour! But the organiser had a point. Bare skin made capture much more hazardous.

Less energetic was the game which came to be known as nine men's morris. It was played outdoors by cutting the shape of nine squares into turf with a sharp knife and providing each of two contestants with three large flat stones, or similar, to use as counters. An indoor adaptation, or one for use at fairs and fetes, would see the nine squares marked out on a board. The aim of each player as he took his turn was to get his three counters all in a row, across, down or diagonally, while his rival strove to intercept him by thrusting his own counter or stone somewhere along that line and hopefully, gain an unbroken row for himself. Black Country winners called out 'tit tat tow – all in a row!' at the moment of triumph. Played as an impromptu table game with pencil and paper, we now know it as noughts (in Staffordshire oughts) and crosses, but a sophisticated boxed version of table top nine men's morris, can be found throughout Britain.

It has to be said that blood sports played a very prominent part in this county in years gone by. Staffordshire men worked hard and played hard and among their more dubious pleasures was animal-baiting. Tutbury in particular gained notoriety for bull-running in the Middle Ages. Amid revelry and music at John of Gaunt's castle the sport was enjoyed by all except the poor creature who was de-horned, de-tailed, grease-smeared and peppered at the nostrils to enrage and make him harder to capture, then to be despatched to some public place and tethered at the mercy of dogs. The Reverend W Beresford, writing in *Memorials of Old Staffordshire*, blames this barbarous sport on the marriage of John of Gaunt and his desire to make his bride, Princess (later Queen) Isabella of Castile, feel at home in Tutbury castle. Happily for the bulls, this custom ceased in 1788, except for the odd bouts arranged 'on the quiet'.

Later more common sports of dog and cock fights brought the county renown before they spread to London and other centres. Up to a generation ago Black Country men saw nothing wrong in these. Though Staffordshire bull terriers were their household pets, they thought nothing of subjecting them to the ordeal of a fight when the 'odds' were right.

Willenhall became especially noted for these contests which were enthusiastically extolled by none other than the Reverend William Moreton, vicar of its largest church, St Giles. But as he was a reprobate, well known for hard drinking and foul language, his approval was of dubious value. How he had the gall to stand up in his pulpit week after week for 45 years (he was appointed in 1788) is a mystery. He must have developed the skin of a rhinoceros when reading from Holy Writ; he could preach with all the fervour of a righteous evangelist, and unashamedly encourage bear baiting as well as the more popular dog fights.

Darlaston as well as Willenhall became noted for the contests which were taken very seriously. Two dogs of equal weight must be selected, the referee appointed, stakes agreed, bets placed and venue chosen. Immediately before the match the animals were washed in milk to ensure that they bore no offputting taste which might have been smeared on by accident or design to discourage an opponent's tongue and teeth. Then, released from

16

respective corners, battle commenced – lasting up to half an hour in some cases before one animal flopped through weariness, or worse. If not too seriously affected, both would be washed and set off again.

Cockfighting, bad as it may have been, seems slightly less brutal. Despite the grim purpose for which the birds were being bred, families actually grew fond enough of their cocks to name them and give them house room in some cupboard or container indoors. They were let out at intervals for an airing – one by one, to discourage rehearsals! Wednesbury and Walsall were known centres for cockfighting, but it, too, became illegal early in the 1900s.

Phil Drabble tells the tale in his excellent book on Staffordshire of a group who sought a venue for an illegal cockfighting bout. They chose a long room over the bar of the Cross Keys in Hednesford, but just before they arrived it had been found necessary to bring the body of a pit casualty to lie therein while awaiting an inquest. However, they were allowed to enter the room to pay their last respects to their late comrade. Could they be blamed for contemplating that in his time the departed one had been a true sportsman who, in similar circumstances, would not have considered it disrespectful to proceed? By common consent they stealthily moved aside the bier, staged the cockfight – and apparently not a soul objected.

Rabbit coursing, whippet racing, rat pits and pigeon fancying all had their enthusiasts. No trouble was too great to spend in training. When it was discovered that pigeons could be induced to fly low (apparently by exploiting the mating urge) it was even possible to race them over a predetermined course against whippets streaking along below. The unpredictability of such a bizarre contest must have aroused nail-biting suspense in the incurable gamblers.

Black Country citizens were tough men who were also hard on themselves when it came to prize fighting and fisticuffs. In addition to routine bouts in the ring, some had been known to climb into a tub, two at a time, to batter each other with bare fists!

17

Perhaps unique to this county – and a 'genteel' contrast to
the hardy sports referred to above – was the activity of the
Staffordshire Otter Hunt along the banks of the river Trent.
This was a serious group of dedicated, patient sportsmen who
converged on Handsacre village, dressed alike in gold-buttoned
blue blazers, grey plus fours, red stockings and sporting red
ties. Sixty years ago a Wolverhampton *Express and Star* journalist
wrote of the soldierly, disciplined bearing of the then Master
of the Hunt, Major D Atkinson. His blazer bore some
additional insignia of office, and hanging around his neck was
a copper hunting horn. All jackets or caps were adorned with
a grisly kind of talisman – an otter's paw mounted on a silver
pin signifying past victories, and each huntsman carried a long
pole.

At the master's signal, out of a black van tumbled fox-
hounds, Welsh hounds and cross-bred otter hounds – 'thirteen
and a half couples', reported 'Quaestor' the newspaper man,
each answering to their names at the Major's call and speeding
down to the riverside followed by three excitable little Sealyham
terriers. The otter gave off a scent which set the hounds in swift
pursuit, but the pace at which their quarry moved over land
and water gave him a sporting chance. The journalist joined
the huntsmen as the party moved off upstream toward Rugeley,
the master and second whip along one side of the river, with
the first whip leading followers on the opposite bank. Despite
his reservations 'Quaestor' caught the thrill of the chase and
only half regretted that he witnessed no kill, for a summer day
among banks, rushes, meadows and bridges had been well spent
in some of the loveliest of the Staffordshire countryside.

Roaring Meg and Singing Kate

AS the passenger coach drew up at the gate of Rushton
Grange on a chilly November day in 1647 a young woman
alighted and glanced up at the country farmhouse which was
to be her home for the foreseeable future. The coachman
deposited her trunk at the door and resumed his journey to
Burslem a few miles farther on.

Today life was beginning anew for the young passenger who
had been engaged to assist in the care of the Biddulph children.
Soon she was inside the bedroom near the nursery which had
been allocated to her, where her trunk had been carried by one
of the domestics. She stooped to pull away the straps, open the
lid and survey its neatly folded contents. What should she wear
for her first evening with the family? She made her choice,
reached in for the garment she wanted – and never knew that
the simple action was to trigger off a traumatic chain of events
involving the whole of Burslem. A subtle, unseen enemy lurked
between the folded layers within her trunk.

Soon she was being introduced to her new charges. Their
father, Francis Biddulph, had known better days before the Civil
War. That terrible conflict had ended the year before, changing
the fortunes of many Royalist families. Rushton Grange was
an unusually modest home for an ancient family like the
Biddulphs of Biddulph Hall. At one time the grange had served
only as a country retreat or guest house, sheltering persecuted
Catholics in times of religious intolerance. The family, by

tradition, held to the old faith and even now, in their reduced circumstances, a priest was in residence.

Francis had inherited the Biddulph estate from his father, John, who had joined forces with Charles I when the Civil War broke out. John had lost his life at Hopton Heath. Francis himself, in his mid 20s and already the father of two children, also enlisted in the Royalist cause. Biddulph Hall was well built and fairly defensible so Francis left the property and his family in the hands of Lord Brereton, who brought his own wife and child under the same roof. The Breretons' home in Cheshire had seemed more at risk. But when the enemy (ironically commanded by Lord Brereton's own uncle) attacked Biddulph Hall with a menacing weapon called 'Roaring Meg' Lord Brereton capitulated. The occupants were saved but the lovely hall was systematically destroyed to prevent it ever becoming a Royalist stronghold.

Meanwhile Francis Biddulph fought on with the Cavaliers and was taken prisoner at Chester. After two years custody in Eccleshall castle he returned home to very reduced circumstances. The grange, the estate farm, was now the home of the family, but Francis maintained them in reasonable comfort, together with some domestic staff, the Catholic priest and an Italian governess who had come to be known in the district as Singing Kate because of her exceptionally beautiful and powerful voice. It seems that she had often been heard out of doors, perhaps practising, or just for the joy of it. This, then, was the household which the young traveller joined on that cold November night.

Within days, if not hours, disaster struck! First the governess, then one after another of the children became violently ill. The dreaded Bubonic Plague raging at what had seemed a safe distance away, had struck them down! The terrible contagion had travelled to Rushton Grange in that neatly packed trunk now stored in the newcomer's room alongside the nursery.

Poor Francis Biddulph was frantic with fear. He rode 40 miles that night in search of a doctor, and everywhere he went he left a touch of the deadly virus. He returned home in near

20

despair. Singing Kate was the first to die, followed at intervals by others. Every precaution was taken, but the plague spread and gripped Burslem. Many died and the fearsome cry 'bring out your dead!' echoed around the hushed streets. Because the plague had broken out at the grange, the Biddulphs were blamed and Francis was at his wits end to obtain supplies while the sufferers lived.

When all was over Francis and his remaining son left the stricken home for London where, in course of time, the son married.

Years later a trench at the back of the hall was discovered to be the burial pit of the Biddulph household in 1647. Shunned when the outbreak was traced to them, it seems they were also denied burial in the churchyard and the survivors would have had the sad task of cleaving the wintry ground. Fortunately the resident priest, with whom a strong bond had been forged, survived to provide a simple burial service. Hopefully Francis gained some consolation from the faith which had sustained past generations of Biddulphs in grief and tragedy.

The burial trench was known in after years as 'Kate's Hole', which has a macabre ring about it. But the nickname of 'Singing Kate' is appealing and the echo of that lovely voice must have lingered on, as song will do, in the hearts and minds of survivors when merciful time began its healing work.

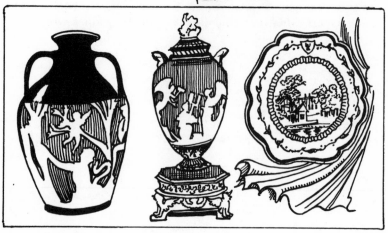

Potbanks and Panorama

IN the summer of 1730 when Josiah Wedgwood first opened his clear blue eyes upon the busy, smoky world at Burslem, there were no less than 43 'potbanks' in existence in that area. His father ran one of them from the family home, with rough workshops behind the living quarters. Because of the plentiful supply of clay, and of the coal to fire it, pot works had existed in that area for 200 years past.

Many were small businesses like that of Josiah's father, handed down through several generations to men who would scour the area for clay and dig it out regardless of the deep pot-holes left behind. This made the rough tracks impassable to wheeled vehicles, but as the men used packhorses or simply humped loads upon their own backs, all that mattered to them was to bring back clay and coal, get on with the job, and produce almost identical products in stone ware, mottled ware, butter pots, simple cottage ornaments and household goods.

At the time of Josiah's birth the business in the churchyard works was run down, barely providing for the large family. Josiah was the twelfth child (though five had died in infancy) so it is unlikely that the new arrival would have been greeted with much ceremony.

When Josiah was only nine years old, his father died, so his brief education ended abruptly. The boy had to make himself useful around the works until old enough to be apprenticed to Tom, the eldest son, who inherited the business. By that time it was insolvent. Had it not been for the legacy left to Tom by a childless aunt, the future for the family would have been bleak indeed.

Josiah was 14 when his apprenticeship was drawn up and his natural flare for the potter's craft emerged. But he was to fight appalling bouts of ill health, even in childhood. Smallpox left him with facial blemishes and stiffness in one knee which affected his ability to work the treadle on his machine. The skill in his hands and the vision in his active brain drove him to try, but it became necessary for others to provide the footwork.

Could this handicap have been the reason why big brother Thomas refused the 19 year old a partnership after he had served the five years' apprenticeship? Swallowing his disappointment, Josiah took the £10 Aunt Kate had left him (Thomas having inherited almost everything else) and went elsewhere. Fortunately he found a partner who was likeminded in seeking to produce wares of superior quality. Here Josiah fashioned the moulds and models while his facile mind worked on new ideas as he travelled to surrounding areas on business.

Then illness struck again. It lasted many months and Josiah languished in lodgings above a draper's shop at Fenton. But not all was lost. The young master potter read avidly from books brought to him by his mother, his sisters and 22 year old cousin, Sarah. She became deeply attached to him despite disapproval from her father, a 'better off' Wedgwood. Meanwhile those hours of reading were eventually to pay great dividends. Josiah's knee became permanently disabled and though possessing an outstanding skill as a potter, his future would depend upon employing others for the manual tasks. His health made it essential that he should now become answerable to no one but himself.

So Josiah returned to Burslem to open up on his own and be free to study new glazes, new mixes, new colours, and exciting innovations which had begun to alarm his former partner by their boldness.

Courageously Josiah leased Ivy House for £10 a year – a home with two-storey workshops built around a rear courtyard. Ambition was spurred on by an ultimatum from cousin Sarah's father. Josiah's proposal of marriage would be considered when he could match equally her dowry of £4,000! It took him seven

24

years to win his bride – it has a biblical ring about it!

On January 25th 1764, despite an accident to his damaged knee causing another devastating spell of illness, Josiah attained that goal. Complete with her bouquet of holly and Christmas roses, Sarah joined him at the altar of Astbury church, and set up home with him.

Josiah's business had expanded far beyond that of his brother, despite Tom's advantage from their aunt's legacy. Josiah moved with the times, playing a vital role in new discoveries and advances – the advent of the steam engine, the building of roads over potholed tracks and, above all, sharing in the planning of the Grand Trunk Canal to economise on transport and bring prosperity to the Potteries.

Could anyone then living in the Potteries ever forget the opening of the canal? Proclaimed a general holiday, crowds converged upon the scene from early morning. Singing, speeches, and toasting brought the moment when Josiah thrust the spade into the soil and swung the first clod into a waiting barrow to be ceremoniously wheeled off by the designer, James Brindley. Cheers heralded feasting and fun. The Leopard Hotel catered for celebrities and the delicious aroma of roasting sheep stirred the anticipation of crowds milling around outside. Parties and bonfires led to the evening street dancing outside Josiah's home to round off that wonderful day.

Inevitably the 33 years that followed the marriage brought fluctuations of fortune to the Wedgwoods. It was a red letter day when they opened a showroom in London, aided by the co-operation of John Wedgwood, an elder brother, who was to represent the pottery in the capital. Royal patronage graced the premises and they were allowed to name their cream earthenware 'Queensware'. But heartbreak also lurked in the capital. Brother John met a mysterious death in the river Thames one dark night, almost certainly at the hands of pickpockets who roamed London streets. It was a sad end to the family tie and Josiah felt it deeply.

In that very week Sarah was brought to bed with the birth of their third child. Then trouble flared up again in Josiah's infected leg until he could not even walk. It became inevitable that he must lose the limb which had troubled him for so long.

In an age when amputations were fraught with danger, the patient faced the ordeal bravely, in his own home. With no anaesthetic except laudanum, it is on record that Josiah actually watched the process which would maim him for the rest of his days. He was only 37 years old, and knew his life would hang in the balance for several days. Unknown to him, during that time Sarah had to cope with the death and burial of one year old Richard. But to her relief Josiah was spared, to be fitted with an artificial limb.

After this harassing year, a close friend joined him in his business. Thomas Bentley moved to London to fill brother John's place. The friendship was a boon. Trouble with his eyesight caused Josiah to fear eventual blindness and it was to Bentley he wrote 'I am practising to see with my fingers . . . but I shall make a wretched walker in the dark with a single leg.'

Fortunately that threat passed. Soon Josiah was on course again, backed by Bentley's friendship, a stable home life and a growing family. It is affecting to find that Josiah's delight in his firstborn (a daughter) was never eclipsed even by the advent of sons who might follow in their father's footsteps. Susannah remained his 'beloved Sukey' with whom he could scarcely bring himself to part even when her hand was sought in marriage by Dr Robert Darwin, the son of a very close family friend. The couple had to wait for years!

The sons born to Josiah and Sarah were welcomed, though not forced, into the pottery enterprise as prosperity advanced. Prestige and success followed the enormous impact made upon the public by Josiah's greatest commission – the order from Catherine, the Empress of all the Russias. The 952 pieces, comprising one dinner service, were laid out in the London showroom in Greek Street, Soho. Only ticket holders were allowed in to the display which spread over five rooms on two floors. The carriages of the rich and famous queued up outside.

What was so special about this tremendous order was that each piece carried the image of a different country house or estate in England. The owners of those (mostly palatial) homes were among the favoured ticket holders, and Josiah indulged himself by one mark of pride. A large oval dish depicted his own new home, Etruria Hall, and skilfully but unobtrusively included the adjoining Etruria Works – the new model factory where all this magnificent ware had been crafted. No matter that the profit margin was slender! The prestige (once the nail-biting commission had been accomplished) was enormous. In all, there were 1,224 views – a wonderful panorama of English country life to grace the royal table in the Chesmenski Palace.

There were other exciting projects, too – the copy of the ancient Portland Vase, for example, so called because it was the Duke of Portland who loaned it to Josiah to attempt making a copy. It featured white cameo figures on dark glass. It had been excavated from a tomb near Rome and was reputed to have held the ashes of the Emperor Alexander Severus. So important was this difficult and prestigious task that Josiah turned for advice to Sir William Hamilton who had been British Ambassador to the Court of Naples and was an authority on antiquities. When the copy had been completed Sir William visited Etruria and penned a verdict which delighted Josiah: 'The sublime character of the original is wonderfully preserved in your copy . . . I give you the greatest credit for having arrived so near the imitation of what I believe to be the first specimen of the excellence of the Ancient Arts existing.'

During those busy years Josiah gained a hearing in Parliament as President of the Chamber of Manufacturers, and, among other reforms, urged the abolition of slavery. He crafted a medallion at the pottery, depicting a manacled slave kneeling to plead his own cause. It spoke louder than speeches with its eloquent caption: 'Am I not a man and a brother?'

The master potter had come a long way. His 64 (often painfilled) years hopefully brought him fulfilment – outstanding success in his chosen career, transforming the industry from the commonplace into the sphere of art and beauty, and the provision of a model village for workers' homes at Etruria. His family were well provided for, and he enjoyed the respect and

27

companionship of men of influence and ideas.

Before the advent of his last, wearying illness in 1794, Josiah brought his sons into partnership, though they had developed other interests also. Then an apparent toothache developed into something more malignant and he could no longer fight his pain. The family came together for a rather sober Christmas that year, and a week later Josiah bade them goodnight for the last time. His bedroom door was locked next morning, so it was the sad duty of the carpenter to fix a ladder to his window and bring the news that his life had ended, apparently peacefully in sleep.

The
'Might-have-been'
Queen

WHEN George Granville Leveson-Gower, the first Duke of Sutherland, died it was said of him by Charles Greville 'He was a Leviathan of Wealth, I believe a richer individual never died'. Leveson-Gower's fortune had largely come through his marriage to Elizabeth, the Countess of Sutherland. Through this wealthy heiress he became the first Duke, and also later inherited his father's title as Marquess of Stafford. A life interest from the profits of the Bridgewater Canal, though his uncle, the Duke of Bridgewater, completed his fortune.

In the 19th century the family's London home was Stafford House, which rivalled many of the royal palaces of Europe in splendour. Apart from properties in Scotland and the south, the family possessed two lavishly appointed country seats in Staffordshire. From Trentham and Lilleshall they exercised a powerful influence in the Potteries and Shropshire coal fields and they employed a vast workforce in the West Midlands.

All of this wealth, social position and influence made up the greatest landed estate in Britain. What is so astonishing, therefore, is that a lovely descendant of the family in 1916 was deemed to be 'unsuitable' for marriage to the heir to the throne.

In the summer of 1916 Edward, the Prince of Wales, returned from the squalor and slaughter of trench warfare in France. He was restless and ill at ease. His father looked anxiously for

29

signs that the experiences which Edward himself described in a letter as 'widening his education among all kinds of men' had awakened in him a greater sense of responsibility and understanding than he had shown hitherto. Now in his early 20s, the prince was an attractive young man, of slight build but well proportioned. The khaki uniform became him, the peaked cap seeming to add keenness and purpose to the blue eyes which looked out from so many studio portraits and press photographs. Surely now, hoped George V, he would settle down and form some sensible attachment to a well born girl who would qualify for the demanding role of future Queen of England.

But Edward returned to France at the end of his leave apparently with no romantic association other than a renewal of his liaison with Viscountess Coke. His preference was still for older society women (Marion Coke was 15 years his senior) who were already married to men of wealth and high social position.

However, in December of that year the prince visited an Army hospital in France and encountered a Red Cross nurse seated at the bedside of a seriously injured soldier whom she had been tending without a break for many hours. The identity of the casualty does not seem to have been recorded, but the nurse was the daughter of the 4th Duke of Sutherland, Lady Rosemary Leveson-Gower.

Although the couple could meet only occasionally during the last year and a half of the war, it seems that there was a mutual attraction. By 1918 Edward and Rosemary were in love, according to the Dowager Lady Hardinge of Penshurst, whose husband was assistant private secretary to King George V. Surely the king would welcome into his family this lovely girl with her delightful smile and sense of humour! Of medium height, she was blonde, blue eyed, with an attractive voice. Just a few months older than the prince, Rosemary was the more mature of the two. According to the prince's biographer, Michael Thornton, she confided to Lady Victor Paget, '. . . He's like a child, weak and very irresponsible. But, you know,

I think I could make something of him.' But perhaps it was rash of the heir to the throne to propose to Rosemary before asking his father's consent. The prince was to meet with a sickening blow.

Oh, yes, King George liked the girl herself well enough, but her mother, Millicent, the former Duchess of Sutherland, did not fit the bill as a royal mother-in-law. In five years of widowhood she had enjoyed quite a fling. Within a year of her first husband's death, Millicent had married again, then almost as quickly divorced. Then she had married a third time, to a man with a most unsavoury reputation.

Added to this Rosemary's uncle had brought disgrace upon himself. He was the Earl of Rosslyn who had a similar record of marital misadventures and had wrought financial havoc as a professional gambler. Three times bankrupt, he had lost his fortune and inspired the popular music hall ditty *The Man who Broke the Bank at Monte Carlo*.

Altogether, it was a formidable recital uniting George V and Queen Mary firmly against the marriage with Rosemary.

Not for the first time (and certainly not for the last) Edward bitterly resented the restriction his status demanded. He now had the delicate task of breaking the news to Rosemary, covering the hurtful truth by saying his parents required him to marry a princess from Europe. She retreated from the situation, even when discovering the real reason, with dignity worthy of a queen.

In 1919 she married the Earl of Dudley's son Eric, Viscount Ednam. The prince's gift was a diamond and sapphire brooch, and he remained a close friend of both bride and groom. The Dudleys had traditionally played host to the royal family and Rosemary entered into her new life with complete poise. She bore her husband three sons, the prince being sponsor to the eldest.

Rosemary and the viscount shared a heartbreaking experience. They lost their second son when his little tricycle edged out into a roadway and he was crushed beneath a lorry. Together they laid him in the Garden of Remembrance at

Witley Court in Worcestershire, one of the Dudleys' loveliest homes, and where the Prince of Wales often stayed.

Only eleven years after her marriage Rosemary's own life came to a tragic end in a horrific plane crash and the prince was much affected at the news.

Not much is recorded of Lady Rosemary's life, but an unusual posthumous tribute came from the widower's second wife, the then Countess of Dudley. She herself was something of a wayward society belle, but in her own autobiography she wrote: 'Eric had first been married to an enchanting creature, Lady Rosemary Leveson-Gower'.

Lady Hardinge's husband, George V's private secretary, witnessed the anxiety of the king as his life neared its end and gossip about the Prince of Wales was rife. 'The boy will ruin himself within a year,' he is reported to have groaned. The 'boy' was then over 40 years old! After the old king died Sir Alexander Hardinge became private secretary to his son when he succeeded to the throne as Edward VIII. The Hardinges were closely involved with the drama when Edward finally threw off his royal shackles to marry Wallis Simpson. Ironically, the divorcee's career closely matched that of the Duchess of Sutherland whose conduct had blighted the romance of Lady Rosemary, her daughter.

Into his famous abdication address Edward brought a note of appeal when he spoke of the brother who would succeed him. '. . . And he has one matchless blessing, enjoyed by so many of you and not bestowed on me – a happy home with a wife and children.'

Would history have taken a different turn if King George and Queen Mary had shown more faith in Lady Rosemary?

Kill or Cure?

TIME after time in Staffordshire's past, sufferers must have rated the remedy worse than their disease! By and large, old cures do not make pleasant reading. By present day standards some 'cures' are gruesome and some positively sadistic. But such remedies are part and parcel of the county's past. Perhaps it is well to glance back at them if only to reassure oneself of the privilege of being born in the 20th century?

Take one cure for warts, for instance; it was said that if rubbed against the palm of an executed criminal the warts would disappear. (How would a sufferer have access to the corpse, one wonders?) Perhaps it was easier and less harrowing to employ the alternative remedy – rubbing your wart on to a snail and impaling the poor victim on to a thorn to wither and die, taking your wart with it.

Old remedies for chin cough (whooping cough to some) could only have been taken in pre-RSPCA days. The feet of a live toad, mole or hare were cut off and hung in a bag around the sufferer's neck. The charm was supposed to work when the poor creature expired.

It is difficult to trace the origin of most of these cures, but there seems to be an underlying principle of finding a scapegoat to suffer in one's place. Transferring an illness to plant life seems less offensive – except to a person who is accustomed to talking to plants in a loving manner! However, very few would have objected to making use of a common bramble which had taken root at both ends. A child had to be taken out before sunrise on three successive mornings and passed nine times under and over an arched bramble while chanting the words:

'Under the briar, and over the briar
I wish to leave the chin cough here.'

It would be disappointing if unsuccessful, as there is more than a hint of discomfort in this remedy, especially when the bramble was cut, fashioned into a cross shape, and worn by the sufferer on the breast!

A much simpler remedy, popular in neighbouring counties also, was offered for a stye on the eye, more often called a powk in the Black Country. The stye had to be rubbed with a genuine gold wedding ring. For those who did not possess one, the alternative was to use a piece of stolen beef and bury it afterwards.

A magnet in the pocket might help cure or ward off rheumatism, while others placed faith in a pocketed potato. For nosebleed a familiar remedy (still known today) was to place a key down the patient's back. In a district world-famous for making locks and keys, this would be opportune.

To be touched by the reigning king or queen was once thought to be a source of healing. The well known story of Dr Samuel Johnson being taken to Queen Anne in 1772 by his parents when a child indicates that it was a well respected custom. Whether he was cured of his skin complaint called 'scrofula' is rather doubtful. He was a sick child for years. So much for the King's Evil!

Oddly enough the wheel seems now to have swung full circle. Our present Royal Family turn to commoners for 'fringe' or alternative medicine, suggesting that we have not travelled so far as may be thought from health seekers in the 17th and 18th century!

A Mafia Boss

IF ever a man lived up to his name it was Jonathan Wild. He was born in Wolverhampton in 1682, and his father was a man of honest character, working as a wig maker, but the boy was trained as a buckle maker and soon grew proficient and enterprising. He started his own business and married a local girl who presented him with a child. So far, so good. Then Jonathan grew restless in the provinces, deserted his family and made his way to London to seek his fortune. Soon he was arrested for debt and for four years languished in prison – if that rightly describes an agile mind eagerly imbibing the skills and subtleties of all the rogues around him.

News of his situation may have reached the family at home, but if they hoped for a prodigal's return they were doomed to disappointment. He emerged from gaol a far worse character than when he went in, and turned to a woman of ill repute named Mary Milliner for help on the road to new enterprises. Together they found premises at Cock Lane in Cripplegate which served a dual role as a brothel and a repository for stolen goods.

Soon Wild gravitated into the despicable role of a double dealer, betraying criminals to the police even while buying stolen goods from vagabonds and thieves. He had the vanity to dress in fancy livery with a silver tipped staff calling himself 'The Chief Thief Catcher in England' – while he himself superintended criminal gangs to carry out organised crime. Criminals who would not co-operate were the victims who were earmarked for betrayal to the police. Despite his own load of guilt, he sent them to gaol and to the scaffold without the

slightest compunction. In 1724 he had the effrontery to suggest that he should be made a Freeman of the City of London for such services!

Wild's ingenuity knew no bounds. He set up a lost property office, claiming a reward for detecting goods (which he had ordered stolen in the first place) and restoring them to grateful owners! He trained girls as servants to gain entry into homes and open the way for plundering them, and craftsmen to disguise jewellery and timepieces. He obtained a vessel to ship abroad goods too 'hot' for sale in England. His escapades have filled books and pamphlets.

By now he had put far behind him all memories of home and family, though his fame became so great that rumours must have filtered through from time to time, and it must have been devastating when his honest parents learned that he was finally brought to book, arrested and taken to Newgate prison for the last time. For a while he managed to carry on his nefarious ways even behind bars, but was eventually convicted for charging ten guineas for locating some stolen lace and restoring it to a lady named Catherine Statham. She was the deprived owner of the goods. Wild's ingenious scheme had backfired at last. His infamous career was at an end.

After a failed attempt at suicide 'The Chief Thief Catcher in England' was hanged at Tyburn in 1725 before a crowd which is said to have numbered 200,000! But a final ignominy awaited him a few years later when his skeleton was dug up and exhibited in some peepshow. He had come a long, long way from those uneventful but honest beginnings in Wolverhampton.

The
Lunar Circle

IT all began by accident, or so it seemed at the time, in the early 1770s, and led to a coming together of some of the most brilliant minds, adventurous innovators and near eccentrics of the century. A friendly meeting between Matthew Boulton and Josiah Wedgwood proved so enjoyable that they planned to meet regularly for dinner and discussion. Boulton was a manufacturer of artistic metalware goods, and Wedgwood the famous potter, but both were interested in new techniques and developments. Wedgwood himself invented a pyrometer to measure degrees of heat during firing, also a new composition for mortars and pestles which came into use by chemists worldwide.

Both knew Erasmus Darwin, the local physician who had earned the reputation of being an ingenious philosopher, and he joined them, eagerly convening meetings. Darwin's inspirations included a gold electrometer, an upright windmill, and a tube for room-to-room communication.

They invited Richard Lovell Edgeworth, a young mechanical genius, and the clockmaker John Whitehurst. By the time James Watt and James Keir came south and joined them, unconsciously they had formed an inventors' club. New ideas, practical, impractical or even in the realm of fantasy, thrived in the genial atmosphere of their meetings in Birmingham and Lichfield.

Along came William Small, a physician with a scientific bent.

He was modest about his own attainments but possessed that precious gift, a harmonising influence – invaluable in a group that was attracting men of quite contrasting personalities, social class and background. James Watt and Matthew Boulton, for instance, were so different in temperament that the business partnership they formed might not have survived without backing from other Circle members.

Watt was a pessimist, thin, droop-shouldered, nervous in manner – a contrast to the confident, ebullient Matthew Boulton, but was very much 'his own man' when it came to an argument! Dr Small showed faith in them by investing in the steam engine developments which were replacing watermill and horse power in the Soho Works. These were situated on moorland, described as being 'on the Staffordshire side of Birmingham', where beautiful articles were fashioned in metal, glass, stone and enamel, including mechanical and astronomical clocks for the Russian Empress.

As well as encouraging new enterprises, the group shared each other's problems, scientific, financial and even personal. When Thomas Day moved to Lichfield and joined the group he had the misfortune to be rejected as a suitor by both the attractive Sneyd sisters who were residing at the Bishop's Palace there. Ironically, fellow Circle member Richard Edgeworth managed to wed them both – Honora after the death of Elizabeth.

Day had an awkward, abrasive personality, bent on putting the world to rights. Writing an anti-slavery drama *The Dying Negro* was all very well, but adopting two twelve year old girls to turn them into 'ideal women', with the intention of marrying one, was taking principles a bit too far! Both girls failed his impossible standards but Circle friends were concerned enough to keep an eye open for a wife for him from then on. But incredibly, he found one for himself later – an heiress, no less!

James Brindley, another famous name in industrial history, had only a short association with the Lunar Circle for he died in 1772, but this amazing man who gave England 365 miles of canals had been involved with members' projects for several years past. Known as 'the schemer', he was unprepossessing in appearance (quite a yokel in fact), but a true genius. His every engineering project was a brainchild developed without putting a stroke on paper – no drawings, no calculations, and certainly no ready reckoner in the 18th century!

When Brindley faced a tough problem he simply took to his bed. Hours – or days – later, he arose with the perfect formula in his head. His last commission was the designing and building of the Grand Trunk Canal in collaboration with Josiah Wedgwood, which made a vital contribution to prosperity in the Potteries. He died in his mid fifties worn out, some believe, by overwork.

Another notable member was the theologian Joseph Priestley who had a brilliant mind but was quite an eccentric. Despite a stammer, he spoke in a rapid chatter and moved with a peculiar trotting movement. He also had an odd facial appearance in that his right profile differed completely from that on the left. After coping with pupils at Warrington Academy, he welcomed the chance to fraternise with gifted contemporaries, and Wedgwood organised finance to aid his research into electricity and chemistry. It so happened that both men were elected Fellows of the Royal Society in 1783.

Wedgwood and Priestley had another experience in common. Both were attacked by rioters. In 1783, an outbreak occurred in the Potteries over the rising price of grain. When a consignment docked at Etruria en route for Manchester a mob of about 700 seized the grain and auctioned it among themselves. They then rampaged among houses of the rich, set fire to buildings and marched on the Wedgwood home, Etruria Hall, deaf to all reason. Four of them thundered on the door and demanded food and drink to sustain them while guarding their booty overnight. Josiah was in London but his wife and 17 year old son dealt with them diplomatically and avoided the crisis, apart from some damage to an outhouse at the pottery.

Priestley's position was even more precarious. His role as a Unitarian minister was unpopular, scientific pursuits were suspect and he had a known sympathy with the ongoing French

Revolution. A mob turned up at his church, the New Meeting House in Birmingham, and burned it to the ground. Furnishings in the Old Meeting House were destroyed with axes and crowbars before they set the building alight. Then began the march on Priestley's own home. A courageous friend raced in a chaise to warn him and, with his wife, he fled through the back door to hide in a neighbour's house. They were but 50 yards away when his library and laboratory were destroyed and the house set on fire.

The crowd sought vengeance on other members of the Lunar Circle. Dr Withering was known to support some of Priestley's radical views. His escape was even more dramatic. Hastily donning a workman's garb, he threw into a wagon his most valuable books and mineral specimens, strewed them with hay and sped rapidly away. Fortunately for him the militia arrived in time to save his house.

James Keir feared it was his turn next. When he applied for weapons to attempt to quell the riot, he could get no authority from scared magistrates. When the rioters sent word that they were on their way, Keir had scouts posted in strategic places and deflected them. Not all Circle members favoured radical politics, but they rallied round the victims. Wedgwood took the homeless ones in.

By 1794, when Josiah Wedgwood's last illness overtook him, and other founder members died or moved abroad, something of the heart went out of the Lunar Circle and it began to decline. It had served a wonderful purpose, encouraged important inventions and greatly increased the quality of life for many members.

And the title? Not, as Erasmus Darwin jestingly suggested, a pseudonym for lunatics – but simply because it was wise to hold their meetings on the Monday nearest to the full moon when members could return home in a good light. So much safer when highwaymen and pickpockets lurked on dark corners!

Robin and the Queen
of the Feast

ONE of Staffordshire's most fascinating legendary figures is
the beautiful Clorinda, sometimes called Queen of the
Shepherds, alternatively Queen of the Feast. The second title
becomes her best because reputedly she had a skilful hand with
the bow and played a central role in the celebrations at Tutbury
Fair in its heyday.

Despite her Amazonian image, Clorinda exercised a romantic
appeal, according to a ballad handed down in Staffordshire.
And who should fall victim to her charms but the doughty
Robin Hood!

Many are surprised to hear of Robin's Staffordshire
connections, but local folk will direct tourists to a stone
commemorating his birth on a site at the eastern edge of
Needwood Forest and to a house built on the birthplace
foundations at Loxley, near Bagot's Park. So whenever the
more famous Sherwood Forest became too dangerous for the
outlaw and his merry men, what could be more natural than
for them to ride westwards into the leafy sanctuary of childhood
haunts in Needwood. Local sites such as Robin Hood's Wells
and Robin Hood's Butts testify to the authenticity of his
Staffordshire roots. And what better occasion for a visit 'back
home' than to attend the annual Tutbury Fair?

On the way to the fair the outlaw and the Festival Queen
met, according to a 15th century ballad. (The quaint, ancient
phraseology has since been simplified for us.) Their first

meeting, and an excellent description of the lady opens with
a forest scene when 'the gentlest thief that ever was' is
addressing his assembled band:

> As that word was spoke, Clorinda came by,
>   The queen of the shepherds was she;
> And her gown was of velvet as green as the grass,
>   And her buskin did reach to her knee.

> Her gait it was graceful, her body was straight,
>   And her countenance free from pride;
> A bow in her hand, and a quiver of arrows
>   Hung dangling by her sweet side.

> Her eye-brows were black, ay, and so was her hair
>   And her skin was as smooth as glass;
> Her visage spoke wisdom, and modesty too;
>   Sets with Robin Hood such a lass!

The ballad extends to over 50 verses, proceeding at leisurely
pace for the minstrel's performance, but having introduced
himself Robin courteously invites the lady to sit and rest while
he and his men set off to find meat for her 'within the hour'.
But he is in for a surprise:

> And as we were going towards the green bower,
>   Two hundred good bucks we espy'd;
> She chose out the fattest that was in the herd,
>   And she shot him through side and side.

> By the faith of my body, said bold Robin Hood,
>   I never saw woman like thee;
> Com'st thou from east, or com'st thou from west,
>   Thou needst not beg venison of me.

However, along to my bower you shall go,
    And taste of a forester's meat;
And when we came thither we found as good cheer
    As any man needs for to eat.

For there was hot venison, and warden pies cold,
    Cream clouted, and honey-combs plenty;
And the servitors they were, beside Little John,
    Good yeomen, at least four and twenty.

With that delightful picnic comes love at first sight. Robin
makes a swift proposal – to send for a priest and be married
there and then. Dutifully Clorinda insists that she must honour
her important appointment at the Tutbury Feast but welcomes
Robin to join here there. Then all the usual fun and frolicking
climaxes with wedding bells.

When dinner was ended, sir Roger, the parson
    Of Dubbridge, was sent for in haste;
He brought his mass-book, bade them take hands
    And joyn'd them in marriage full fast.

And when Robin came in sight of the bower,
    Where are my yeoman? said he:
And Little John answer'd, Lo yonder they stand
    All under the greenwood tree.

Then a garland they brought her, two and by two,
    And placed them all on the bride's head:
The music struck up, and we all fell to dance,
    'Till the bride and bridegroom were a-bed.

And that, surely, should be our cue to draw the curtains on
Robin Hood's Staffordshire romance.

'Doctor Doom'

'THERE'S no accounting for tastes!' So runs the familiar retort, and it often applies to human relationships. Whatever is it, for instance, that brings about a special link between a parent and one particular child in a family? This was certainly puzzling in the case of Sarah Palmer's love for her second son, born in 1824. Yet that love survived through unimaginable disasters. Some think it was a contributory cause of them.

Sarah was the wife of Joseph Palmer, a timber merchant of Rugeley. Five more children arrived in the household after young William's birth, but for him that special relationship persisted. The eldest son, Thomas, seems to have been a responsible and caring type of whom any parent might be proud. He had been ordained into the Anglican ministry by the time his father died, leaving him as sole heir to all assets other than ample provision made for Sarah. Thomas then took the unusual, if not unique, step of sharing out equally the legacy of nearly £50,000 – a fair sum in those days.

Despite William, that second brother, showing signs of instability at school and in his teens, he received his £7,000 share like the rest. For him it should have been timely as he left grammar school and embarked on a career in Liverpool, apprenticed to a firm of wholesale druggists. But here a very chequered career began. In a short time he was dismissed for embezzling money which customers had sent through the post with orders.

William returned home and his mother, by now a rather merry widow enjoying her freedom, managed to cover for him

and get him a second apprenticeship, this time to a surgeon in Heywood, nearer home. But this also ended abruptly when he was discovered to be getting along with female patients, not wisely but too well! And the misdemeanours were being compounded by further dishonesty to cover gambling debts. Somehow he avoided public exposure by absconding.

Palmer's next and apparently more successful training began at the Stafford Infirmary and led on to medical studies at the famous St Bartholomew's in London. Here, in 1846, he qualified as a member of the Royal College of Surgeons and was offered an appointment on Bart's medical staff. But he preferred to return to Rugeley and set up in practice. As the brass plate carrying his credentials went up, his family must have happily concluded that all his wild oats had been sown.

In the following year he was married to 18 year old Anne Brookes of Stafford. She felt flattered by the proposal of a young, flamboyant doctor, though her guardian was not so sure about him. But Anne carried the stigma of illegitimacy and though her father acknowledged her, and had made some future provision for her, she was anxious to change her name and status.

Poor girl – she was to pay dearly for it. She bore five children in quick succession and only the eldest lived beyond infancy, while the doctor was spending more time philandering and on the racecourse than in surgery. The lure of the turf had returned. His professional status brought him into society which encouraged him to dabble in racehorse ownership as well as gambling. Debts mounted. So did threats from dealers and bookmakers, and events took a sinister turn.

The four infant mortalities, and the death of an illegitimate child of Palmer's, had not been satisfactorily explained, though an aged family doctor (who had brought Palmer himself into the world) made no bones about signing certificates. Then Anne's father died and Palmer invited his now 'comfortably off' mother in law to join the family. She was ill within a week and died soon afterwards, despite the old family doctor's prescription.

With a debt of £800 hanging over him, Palmer invited the creditor, Leonard Bladen, to break his journey home from Chester Races, ostensibly to collect his debt and stay under the Palmers' hospitable roof. He consented, and died within three days, the aged Doctor Bamford obliging with the certificate. Bladen's betting book mysteriously disappeared and Palmer brazenly claimed that Bladen was, in fact, in his debt!

Temporarily relieved, Palmer went deeper into debt. He insured Anne's life for £1,300 and she died after payment of the first premium. Bamford and another elderly doctor certified death through 'bilious cholera'.

Palmer's brother Walter drank heavily. Palmer insured him for a similar amount and gave him into the care of a nursing couple. Would nature take its course? It did so rather too slowly. William called at a chemist's shop en route to visiting his sick, alcoholic brother. Two days later Walter died.

This time the Insurance Company was not quite so quick to pay out. While they deliberated, Palmer got desperate and accompanied a racing friend, John Cook, to Shrewsbury Races to see Cook's horse 'Polestar' run. The horse came in first and Cook won £2,500, receiving £800 on the course with the balance payable on the following Monday from Tattersalls. After the races the two men stayed one night at a hotel and Cook became unwell. They then returned to Rugeley where Cook stayed at the Talbot Arms – visited frequently by his 'friend', bearing medical advice and nourishment. The illness worsened over the next two or three days, and the young doctor watched as Cook endured excruciating pain. Elderly Dr Bamford attended him, and was joined by a doctor friend of Cook's own. Nevertheless after some fluctuation in the symptoms of his illness John Cook died in the early hours of the morning five days after Shrewsbury Races. Needless to say, the £800 had disappeared together with the betting books, and the £1,700 had been obligingly collected from Tattersalls by a 'friend'.

Before Dr Palmer could get the body removed Cook's stepfather arrived on the scene – and the curtain began to fall on this Greek tragedy. The post mortem which he demanded

48

erupted in chaos. A morbid group of onlookers including the hotel landlord and the postmaster gained entry into the dissecting room (where the victim died). Dr Palmer was also present. The Stafford doctor who was to supervise the work (carried out by a medical student and a doctor's dispensary assistant) forgot his instruments – and scissors had to be used! Vital samples were spilled when the dispensary man got inebriated and half stumbled against his working partner. Or was he pushed, as the Stafford supervisor asserted later? Palmer tried to bribe the postboy, as he left for Guy's Hospital, to drop the jar which contained the stomach contents – and actually succeeded in getting the postmaster (an old schoolfellow) to open the laboratory's report from Guy's when it came back.

As Palmer had hoped, little or nothing could be deduced from the damaged samples sent from the bodged autopsy. But the respite was brief. There were some traces of poison. A properly conducted inquest must now follow. Chickens were coming home to roost with a vengeance. A week later William Palmer was in Stafford Gaol, charged with the murder of John Cook! The bodies of Palmer's wife and brother were exhumed. Poison was traced and verdicts of 'Wilful Murder by William Palmer' were announced by the Coroner.

Murder is always cruel, but poison is surely the most calculated and merciless weapon of all. Palmer witnessed the suffering of his victims, yet persisted in administering the doses. Feelings ran so high in Staffordshire that Palmer was hurried to London and the sensational trial for the murder of John Cook was held amid enormous publicity at the Central Criminal Court on 14th May 1856. The courtroom was crowded to capacity.

Certain though the prosecution was of the doctor's guilt, it took many hours of professional expertise to build up the case on what had to be circumstantial evidence. The judge's summing up was emphatically against the prisoner and after twelve epic days, a verdict of guilty was announced and the solemn ceremony of the death sentence followed. The two other cases were left 'on file'. Speculation was rife, of course, about

49

all those other unexplained deaths and many incidental offences including fraud, robbery, and forgery. But the prisoner had only one life to forfeit and about 25,000 hostile spectators turned up on the 14th June – some from as far afield as the Continent – to watch the 31 year old Rugeley doctor (who never admitted to the crimes) die on the scaffold outside Stafford Gaol.

And what of the mother whose favourite son this was? She was herself the victim of some of his forgeries when he sought access to her assets. Yet, even so, Sarah Palmer may have been the author of the protest contained in 'A Letter to the Lord Chief Justice Campbell' published in London soon after the trial, and complaining of his summing up. On the frontispiece it carried the name of the evil doctor's clergyman brother, though Thomas denied its authorship. Some years later William's mother was heard to sigh 'I had seven children and my saintly Bill was the best of the lot!'

The Captive Queen

THE role of a gaoler is not a happy one, unless he be a sadist. This the Earl of Shrewsbury was not, and he found himself in deep waters when his Sovereign, Elizabeth I, laid upon his unwilling shoulders the custody of her wayward cousin Mary, Queen of Scots. How was this courtly English peer to balance restraint with the respect due to a royal personage? Receiving insufficient financial provision for the task, he walked a tightrope. If too parsimonious, he risked the displeasure of Queen Elizabeth. And if too generous, his formidable wife – the renowned Bess of Hardwick – roundly accused him of being in love with his beautiful 27 year old prisoner with her celebrated charm. It was, as they say today, a 'no win' situation from the moment he collected his charge at the Scottish border on a bleak January day in 1569 and brought her south into Staffordshire where she was to spend many of her remaining 19 years.

Mary had looked for refuge with her cousin, Elizabeth, but her past history of misrule with lurid love affairs provoking jealousy, intrigue and murder, did not commend itself to the Virgin Queen. More importantly, Mary's presence posed a threat to Elizabeth's throne as long as Catholic supporters strove to advance her cause and enhance her status. So the hunting lodge at Tutbury went some way to minimise illusions of grandeur. The castle, now a Crown possession leased to the Earl, once housed a Queen of Castile (the bride of an heir) with

51

glittering splendour in its heyday. Now it was damp, neglected and malodorous with bad sanitation.

The Scottish Queen was dismayed, even outraged, at such accommodation 'for a person of my quality'. But protests were in vain and she composed herself to bide her time and maintain the charm which had hitherto proved irresistible to powerful men. Thirty two year old Thomas, Duke of Norfolk, came trotting blithely across the moat bridge one day and was her first conquest. He proposed marriage and a rescue plan. Norfolk was the leading Catholic in England, so he should have trodden very softly under Elizabeth. But his heart ruled his head. The romance and plan were detected, and Norfolk despatched to the Tower. Even so, Mary managed to send coded letters to him in empty beer bottles hidden among a crate of full ones, and distinguished by secretly marked corks. Love found a way, it seems, though not to the freedom Mary longed for, nor did it save Norfolk from execution on Tower Hill.

The winter that followed was a bitter one for the Queen of Scots in more ways than one. The damp accommodation brought on rheumatics and she begged for a move. The Earl was allowed to take her to Wingfield Manor in Derbyshire temporarily, but in early summer she was back at Tutbury, consoled by the promise of some outdoor sport which she loved. Over the next 12 or 13 years a round of gaols and two changes of gaoler may have relieved the monotony of imprisonment to some extent. But back she came to Tutbury in 1585 for the fourth time with Sir Ralph Sadler in charge, allowing a little more leniency and a larger band of attendants. Judging by household records, they were also better fed. At one time she was reported to have a stud of 16 horses, two dogs, turtle doves and Barbary fowls. When indoors, needlework whiled away the day and months.

But such is human nature – Catholic friends took advantage of this regime and Elizabeth, fearing trouble, replaced Sir Ralph with a younger, zealous Protestant gaoler. He conveyed her to Chartley Castle, utterly regardless of the protests of its owner, the young Earl of Essex.

The Chartley move was surprising because the castle was more vulnerable to incursions from outsiders than were Mary's usual gaols. Later it transpired that the move was probably designed to lull Mary into a false sense of security and trap possible rescuers. If so, it succeeded. Whilst Mary was allowed out with a hunting party at Tixall, a vigorous search ensued and the sensational Babington plot was uncovered. This involved collusion between France and Spain in an invasion of England, joining up with English Catholics, murdering Elizabeth and crowning Mary as Queen of England! Anthony Babington has gone down into history as the go-between who was appointed to kill Elizabeth.

Mary returned from the hunt a sick woman, unknowingly facing the greatest threat she had yet encountered. Her gaolers interrogated her on her sick bed, got nothing in the way of a confession, yet took her away to face her doom. She left Staffordshire, probably without regret, for the last time in September 1586, arrived at Fotheringhay and faced incredible odds in a trial for her life. Though still beautiful, having what an admirer called 'an alluring grace, pretty Scotch speech and a searching wit', the odds were laid too heavily against her.

Nineteen years after meeting her at the Scottish border for the first time, it was the Earl of Shrewsbury who broke to her the news of the verdict and the death sentence. Next morning, with dignity and courage, she bowed her head to the block in that castle.

Some Staffordshire folk regret that the county's reputation for providing sanctuary was impaired by the Scottish queen's treatment at Tutbury and Chartley. But how pleasing it is to reflect that at least it did not provide the venue for that last macabre exhibition.

Staffordshire's Taj Mahal

IT must have been a delightful occasion when the Hon Emily
Charlotte Wood, daughter of the 1st Viscount Halifax, was
married to Hugo Francis Meynell Ingram in 1863. The
Meynells were a distinguished Staffordshire family who had
been involved in England's history since fighting at Crecy and
Poitiers. But what was especially pleasing about this 'good
match' is that it was firmly based on mutual love, as events
were to prove.

After the wedding Hugo brought his young bride to Hoar
Cross Hall in Needwood Forest where his father was squire and
master of the Meynell Hunt. Soon Emily joined her mother-
in-law, playing a central role in village affairs. Hugo's favourite
sister, Louisa Elizabeth, would have provided good company.
Known locally as 'Missy' she was a popular member of the
family.

Most of the Hoar Cross villagers worked for the Meynells
in one capacity or another – at the hall itself, on the estate
or in the big complex of stables and kennels. It speaks volumes
for the relationship between squire and villagers to read that
all who could get on horseback were free to follow the hounds
and enjoy an exciting day in the field. Two or three generations
back it had been a Meynell who was named the 'Father of
Foxhunting' and since then much of the life of the village had
revolved around the sporting fraternity in the area and in
Yorkshire where the Meynells had another estate. This, of

course, would lead to a good deal of fraternising with County families and entertaining at the hall, so it was into a lively, prosperous household that Hugo's young bride settled.

Inevitably, time brings change to every family. In the Meynells' case, it happened all too quickly. The old squire's wife died in 1868 and his death followed four months later, in February 1869. Management of the estate and hunt fell upon Hugo's shoulders and of course Emily was now the 'squire's lady'. But little more than a year later Hugo suffered a serious accident in the hunting field, and at the end of the same year (1870) the lively, favourite sister of the family died. Three months later Hugo himself died leaving his young wife childless and Hoar Cross Hall without an heir to carry on the splendid old name.

The young widow must have been devastated. How silent and empty the family home must have seemed in a short space of time. Even the stables and kennels fell empty for a new hunt master had to take over and horses and hounds went to nearby Sudbury. But happily, Emily's own family rallied to her aid. The elder brother, Charles, had inherited the Halifax title and estate, but her younger brother, 25 year old Frederick, came to join his widowed sister at Hoar Cross Hall. His help and support was invaluable. He settled in well at Hoar Cross, becoming High Sheriff of the county in time, and generously joining his sister in what now became her paramount ambition – honouring Hugo's memory and perpetuating his family name. In all the 33 years that were ahead of her, she dedicated herself unreservedly to devising a worthy memorial.

That memorial, the Church of the Holy Angels in Hoar Cross, was to become renowned for its beauty and its wealth of unusual features. It is described as the most beautiful of its type to be found in all England and Arthur Mee calls it 'a little Cathedral'. From all over the globe travellers have found their way to the clearing in Needwood Forest to see it for themselves. Surely it must rank with the famous Taj Mahal as a monument to enduring love.

Mrs Meynell Ingram chose an architect from Liverpool

Cathedral to design the church in rich red sandstone with a central tower rising 110 ft high over the lawn. Nothing was hurried; nothing was scamped. Throughout the four years of its erection, the foundress took a keen personal interest, almost on a day to day basis, and even when the main structure and interior were completed and opened she continued, as the years went on, to find and add yet more touches of beauty and individuality.

It is heartening to find that the young widow did not hide herself away in morbid contemplation. She is described as being gifted intellectually, deeply spiritual and must also have been an outgoing personality. When travelling overseas she turned every excursion into a voyage of discovery keeping a lookout for new ideas, new methods, or new crafts to add lustre to her great enterprise at Hoar Cross.

While cruising off the Baltic coast in her yacht she disembarked at Danzig, toured round the Marienkirche, learned of a new colouring process there and somehow coaxed the secret out of the artists to bring the formula back to Hoar Cross. It was used to beautify the figures enclosed in carved wooden panels depicting the 14 Stations of the Cross. This carving was carried out by two aged craftsmen brought over from Antwerp. Maybe they were coaxed aboard the yacht on a homeward journey! It was almost their last work and is a worthy tribute to their skill.

Also from the Continent (The Convent of San Marco in Florence) came an ivory crucifix of exceptional beauty to be placed in what was to become Hugo's resting place, the chantry chapel. Also in the chantry may be found carvings which include the entire range of musical instruments listed in the Scriptures. There are countless lovely examples of skilled craftsmanship in stone, glass, metal and woodwork. Beautiful windows present a veritable picture gallery. Slender pillars, arches and canopies all over the building support the figures of hosts of angels, as befits the name of this church. Many lovely features outside and within the building have journalists and reporters vying with each other for adequate words.

What a marvellous day it must have been in 1874 when the Bishop of Lichfield came to celebrate Holy Communion and institute the first vicar. This was no mausoleum. It was a living, thriving village church open to all who would come. On that Dedication Day visitors from far and near must have been enchanted by the fulfilment of the young widow's dream.

The body of the young squire was brought from its temporary plot to the beautiful chantry chapel. The alabaster figure representing him is clothed in the uniform of the Staffordshire Yeomanry, with a hound lying at his feet. Carved angelic figures watch overhead beneath a richly sculptured canopy of stone.

Twelve years into her widowhood the foundress turned her thoughts to the plight of parentless children and opened part of her home as a private orphanage. The sound of children's voices must have enlivened the hall. But it was mainly the companionship and loyal support of her brother, Frederick, which kept Hoar Cross Hall 'alive' and still the pivot of village life. He married the daughter of the 25th Earl of Crawford and Balcarres, and took the name of Meynell for himself and his family. His sister must have been delighted when he and Lady Mary named their first son Francis Hugo Lindley Meynell.

In 1904, after 33 years of widowhood, came the time for Emily Charlotte to be laid beside her husband in the memorial church. The vacant place was filled and beautified. The white alabaster figure resting tranquilly on a pillow with soft lace drapery reaching her shoulders is said to be a perfect likeness of the foundress, with a model of her little dog at her feet.

The estate now passed to brother Frederick who, dying six years later, was carried to a quite different but splendid tomb alongside the red wilderness wall outside the church itself. As the Hon Frederick George Lindley Meynell, he is sculptured kneeling in his robes of office as High Sheriff and attended by four delicately carved angelic figures. On either side are two memorial tablets, that of his wife Lady Mary Meynell, and the other of their eldest son, Francis Hugo, who died in 1941.

The churchyard has its own beauty, even apart from the

richly sculptured figures placed at intervals. To a departing visitor glancing back on the scene, a burst of late afternoon sunshine will cast an ethereal rosy glow on the church's red sandstone walls, conveying a sense of benediction upon this place of tender memories.

That
'Olde Sweet Song'

DUNMOW in Essex seems to get all the publicity for the custom of awarding a flitch of bacon to any couple who can prove absolute tranquillity during their bridal year, with no regrets for tying the knot. But any good Staffordian will tell you the custom was instituted at Wychnor, a village between Lichfield and Burton-on-Trent, by John of Gaunt in the second half of the 14th century. The Lord of Wychnor was responsible for administering the contest, checking the claims, examining witnesses and superintending the final ceremony of avowal which must be made by every winner. It is almost more impressive than the marriage ceremony itself . . .

> 'Sir Philip de Somerville, lord of Wychnor, maintainer and giver of this bacon, hear ye that I, since I wedded my wife and since I had her in my keeping a year and a day after our marriage would not have changed her for any other, fairer or fouler, richer or poorer, nor for any other descended of greater lineage, sleeping or waking, at any time. And if she were sole and I sole, I would take her to be my wife before all women in the world of what condition soever they be, good or evil, as God help me and all His saints and this flesh and all fleshes.'

The pomp and ceremony which accompanied the award indicates it to be an uncommon event, suitably celebrated. The flitch was presented in the manorial hall, after which the winner was conducted to the outer door with trumps and tabors 'and other manner of minstrelsy'. Once outside, the flitch was laid on a bed of corn on the back of one horse and the winner was despatched on a second mount to the strains of another volley from the musical 'minstrelsy'.

Some humorist writing in *The Spectator* in October 1714 recounted the tale of a number of rejected applicants for the flitch and ended by tracing only two successful ones. One was a sea captain who had not seen his wife from the day of the marriage until the day of the claim. The other turned out to be 'a husband of plain good sense and a peaceable temper'. Was it a coincidence that his wife happened to be dumb? In the 1930s, 'Quaestor', who was on the staff of the Wolverhampton *Express and Star,* went to visit the village to check on the custom. He was directed to Wychnor Hall and glimpsed a life size replica of the flitch hanging over the Jacobean fireplace in the entrance hall. No one had claimed the prize in living memory and he came to the conclusion that the Dunmow flitch had become more celebrated only because Staffordshire men were too honest to lay their claim!

Journalists are notoriously hard to impress, but sometimes even newsprint sparkles with an unexpected glow. The *London Post* of 18th August 1738, carried a delightfully worded announcement:

> 'A few days since the Rev. Mr Harris of Yattingdon, Berks., was married to Miss Nicholls of Stafford, a young lady of great Beauty, an ample fortune, and endowed with all the valuable qualifications of her Sex.'

This must have been 'a marriage made in Heaven'! One can only hope that the parson deserved his good fortune. How appropriate to this marriage would have been the old delightful custom of composing a wedding song, known as an Epithalamium. And if inspiration failed at the right time a verse already composed should have sufficed very well for the Rev. Mr Harris:

'To please, ye votries of Hymen, away,
'Tis yours to be happy when Love crowns the day,

In raptures advance, the appearance to grace,
For all other pleasures to Love must give place,
Then quickly ye Nymphs to the nuptials repair,
With Flora's best presents to welcome the fair.

May such be the man, who deserving the fair,
Of life's daily blessings the choicest may share,
And those real comforts from wedlock arise
Which no friends of harmony too much can beprize.'

Sadly, however, it has to be admitted that not all marriage customs struck such a salubrious note. That relic of feudal tyranny known as the 'droit du Seigneur' or 'merchetum' sends shivers down the spine. It actually claimed the right of the Lord of the manor to take what was delicately phrased as 'the maiden's fee' before a tenant's daughter could be given in marriage. What an intolerable situation! But whether this was actually legal is debatable because one old document records that in the year 1310 Lord John de Heronville was brought before a Court to answer 'certain complaints'. Thankfully this is a relic of the 'good old days' that seems to have been dismissed by law.

A less intimidating, but more widespread, ordeal awaited the bride of a later century – that of 'bedding the newly-wedded couple'. A girl who married a Staffordshire collier had to face up to the indignities with what composure she could muster. This, too, has been put into rhyme in a poem called *The Collier's Wedding:*

'The posset made, the bride is led
In great profusion to her bed;
The females with an edict come
That all the men depart the room.
Thus Nanny Foster caught the bowl
Where currant cakes in ale did roll;
Then, with a smile, said "Jenny, lass,
Come, here's thy health, without a glass."
Her arm supports it to her head;
She drinks and gobbles up the bread;
So every one their courses took –
Some watch for fear the men should look.

Then Tommy next must be undressed,
But which of them can do it best?
    It is no matter, all assist,
Some at his feet, some at his breast;
Soon they undress the jolly blade,
Who into bed is fairly laid . . .'

It does not seem that 'quiet weddings' were the norm in Staffordshire, they were seen rather as occasions for general celebration. In the south of the county it became a sports day for the benefit of the neighbours. Football between rival parish teams was always popular. The ball was presented by the groom but known as a 'bride ball', which seems a little odd. Hopefully this was no indication of his intended treatment of her.

Not all couples relished 'fuss' at their weddings. Some may have had reasons best known to themselves for being bashful, so it must have been a relief when Staffordshire boasted its very own 'Gretna Green' at Norton-in-the-Moors, near Leek. Perhaps it is a pity this ended in 1754 by a special Act which denied such marriages legality – or Staffordshire might have been an even more popular area than it now deservedly is.

Companions of
The River Bank

THE friendship between Izaak Walton and Charles Cotton astonished everyone; they were so far apart in age and temperament. Izaak was an upright man who had won considerable respect in business and as a writer, whereas young Charles was a scamp – there is no other word for it! Yet the rapport between them was so perfect that Cotton was able to add a section to Izaak Walton's famous classic *The Compleat Angler* in just the same style as Walton's own, somewhat on the lines of a theatrical script. Information, instruction, scenic description, poetry and song are provided by means of dialogue between interesting characters devised by the authors. Art and literature combine to make it far more than a tome on angling. As Christopher Harvey put it many years ago:

> 'Here sits, in secret, blest Theology,
> Waited upon by grave Philosophy,
> Both natural and moral: History,
> Deck'd and adorn'd with flowers of Poetry,
> The matter and expression striving which
> Shall most excel in worth, yet not seem rich.'

This unique sporting book has delighted readers for over 300 years. How amazing that such harmony prevailed between men with such different backgrounds.

It was in 1593 that Izaak Walton first saw the light of day

in a village on the Needwood Forest border, near Yoxall. His father died only four years later and after a brief education at Stafford Grammar School, Izaak was sent to London and apprenticed. Some say this was to an ironmonger but his biographer, Sir Harry Nicholas, claims it to have been to a draper. It seems well authenticated that Izaak set up in business as a draper in Fleet Street where he enjoyed the acquaintance of famous men of letters and of the cloth. Dr John Donne, the eminent poet, was his vicar at nearby St Dunstan's church, and here in 1626, he married 19 year old Rachel Floud, a member of the Cranmer family.

How sad that their 14 years together were overshadowed by seven infant deaths, and Rachel died childless. Hopefully Izaak found consolation as well as recreation on the banks of the river Lea, because (to quote his own words in the book that was to follow) 'Angling . . . is an art worthy of the knowledge and practice of a wise man . . . a rest to his mind, a cheerer of his spirits, a diverter of sadness, a calmer of unquiet thoughts, a moderator of passions, a procurer of contentedness . . .'

He was fortunate also in finding another diversion. His literary friends encouraged him in his own writing talent and in 1640, the year following Rachel's death, his first book was published. It was a biography of Dr Donne who had recently died, and its excellent reception encouraged him to follow it with four other brief life stories of famous poets and theologians. His simplicity of style attracted readers. He also began writing verse.

In the early 1640s the victories of Parliamentarians in the Civil War drove many Royalist sympathisers out of London, and Izaak Walton came back to Staffordshire after well over 30 years' exile. He was welcomed and entertained in the homes of clergy and other country gentlemen. Now his sporting skill and love of angling found wonderful scope among the streams and rivers of his native county – the Sow, the Trent, the Severn, the Manifold, the Hamps, the Ouse and the Dove as well as many smaller waterways bearing picturesque rural names. All these and the beautiful moorland scenes of north

Staffordshire must have inspired his work on *The Compleat Angler, or the Contemplative Man's Recreation.*

Life took a happier turn in another direction also. In 1646 Izaak married Anne, a relative of Bishop Ken, and in due time was blessed by the birth of a daughter, also Anne, and a son named after himself. Seven years later, in Izaak's 60th year, the famous angling book was published. The utter simplicity of style and the charm of its contents quickly attracted the reading public and it soon ran into second and third editions.

When Izaak became prosperous he gave a 900 yard plot of land to the poor of Stafford, and bought a 50 acre farm at Shallowford for the family home. At this time he was enjoying the friendship of the Cottons of Beresford Hall, near Hartington, a splendid old mansion overlooking the valley of the river Dove.

This was when Charles, the scapegrace son of that family, eagerly attached himself to his father's friend on fishing expeditions. The senior Cottons must have sighed with relief. Charles had been a thorn in their flesh for years on account of his extravagant living, and was labelled a 'money squanderer'. His debts must have become very heavy; he was in constant fear of pursuing creditors. In a rock near the Beresford bowling green was a crevice into which Charles desperately squeezed when pursuers were descending on the hall. How his parents coped with the embarrassment is not revealed, but there must have come a time when they suffered it, rather than continue to pay their son's debts.

Is it possible that the young Charles had an ulterior motive at the onset of his association with Izaak Walton? Certainly a low stool on an obscure tree-fringed river bank, alongside a respectable elderly companion, sounds a much more agreeable refuge than that crevice in the rock.

It seems that Izaak took Charles under his wing, referring to him as 'Son', but Charles stoutly asserted that the older man (who could have been his grandfather as years count) was 'the best friend I ever knew'. They roamed far and wide over the county, more particularly in the scenic moorland area. They were spoiled for choice as they sampled such streams as the Windrush, the Kennet, the Stour, the Orwell, the Dart and the Tamar, all abounding with 'a variety of fish, later to be lovingly described in the book. The Trent, they declared to be 'one of the finest rivers in the world, and the most abounding with excellent trout and all sorts of delicate fish'.

Izaak became a widower again when he was 70 and so perhaps appreciated all the more the fishing-house which Charles erected for them both on the banks of the Dove. A stone, on which was carved the monogrammed initials of the two men, was conspicuously set in the building and seems to epitomize the harmony. It was when *The Compleat Angler* reached its 5th edition in 1676 that the now 83 year old author requested Charles to expand the book to include 'The Art of Fly Fishing'. This he did in the space of ten days, with such beautiful descriptions of the area and choice selection of 'speaking characters', that Charles earned a well-deserved reputation for himself.

It is safe to assume that youthful indiscretions had long since faded. Whatever Charles Cotton's failings, his long devotion to his best friend seems to prove that the leopard can change his spots. Izaak Walton lived to the age of 90 and was then in the care of his daughter, Anne, and her husband, William Hawkins, a prebendary of Winchester Cathedral. A fine and peaceful setting, one would think, for the last days of this good old man.

A Case
for Sherlock

WHEN the exit door of Portland Prison opened one
autumn day in 1906 a very mystified young man stepped
hesitantly outside and peered around uncertainly. George Edalji
had been sentenced at the Staffordshire Quarter Sessions in 1903
to seven years' penal servitude. Now, suddenly, without a word
of explanation he had been summoned from his prison cell,
conducted to the reception area and presented with his own
belongings to prepare immediately for his return to
Staffordshire. Until the stout door actually closed and locked
behind him, leaving uniformed figures on the other side, he
must have thought someone was playing a sick joke upon him.
And even now, on the outside, he must have blinked fearfully
around, for he was very short sighted, in case some mistake
might suddenly be discovered and his unexpected liberty be lost
again.

Thirty year old Edalji had qualified as a lawyer before his
conviction, and knew that sudden changes of heart just did not
happen in British law. But nobody had thought fit to enlighten
him at Portland, or to answer his hesitant, mystified questions.
But he should have been accustomed to that by now, so he
mechanically followed instructions step by step. Now, for the
first time in three years he had to think for himself and move
on, heading for the railway station as best he could for he felt
nervous even now of stopping strangers to ask the way. A shy
man by nature, he had found to his great cost that his dark

skin and eastern features threw up a barrier between himself and the British though he had been born and bred here.

At the station he handed in his rail voucher for London, the first stage of his journey, found a seat in a third class compartment, and began to breathe a little more easily when the train moved forward and nobody had arrived to challenge his right to be there. He glanced down at the dark suit he had worn at his trial and felt reassured. No one in the compartment should know where he had come from today. He glanced outside and watched the network of rail lines crisscrossing alongside the track as his train gathered momentum, and felt he was on more familiar ground. When studying at college in Birmingham (it was later to become the university) he had written a successful book on railway law which had gained him some recognition and, alongside his prize from the Law Society, helped to launch him on his career. He had started out with such high hopes and his parents had been so proud of him, their eldest son.

But oh, that was long ago and in a different world, or so now it seemed. The train took on the familiar five-beat rhythm and sped him to Paddington. There he located the London and North Western line and was soon speeding westward on the familiar route he had travelled in the past on law business. But the questions ran on unchecked. Law business? How would he stand now if he was indeed free? Could he return to the law practice in Birmingham? Had he been cleared? If not there was no future in the legal profession for him. He would carry the stigma of prison life. He had been disgraced, degraded, forced into unaccustomed manual work in ill-fitting prison garb. He had been thrust into the company of men who despised him for having a darker skin than their own, for being a 'foreigner' higher up the social ladder than themselves, and for the crime of which he had been accused. There are ways of expressing feelings against a fellow prisoner! And all for a crime of which he was completely innocent! A despicable crime, or, rather, series of crimes against dumb animals, of which even a drunken lout might have been ashamed in his better moments.

But the mystery man, who had stooped so low as to cruelly injure and kill helpless animals in the pastureland around Great Wyrley, must have been both heartless and shameless. Those injured creatures . . . it was painful even to recall them now for they had been slashed and left to bleed to death in darkness. It was the work of a sadist – and a racist into the bargain, for he had sent poison pen letters implicating the vicar's son. Moreover he had eluded, goaded and taunted the police time and time again until they had been driven wild enough to arrest somebody – anybody – especially if he had a black skin, be he the devil's advocate or the vicar's son. Racism did not stop with the cruel lout (or louts) responsible for the crimes. The police were only too ready to take note of the hoax letters implicating the vicar's son. They found a handwriting 'expert' who declared them to be in the young lawyer's handwriting – even though the crude wording accused Edalji himself of the crimes!

The police made their arrest, to the astonishment of the suspect's father who had been vicar of the parish at Great Wyrley for 30 years. The Rev Shapurji Edalji was a Parsee who had been converted to the Christian faith and studied for the ministry in England. The Parsees originated from Persia, and were an ancient and distinguished race, but they were dark skinned. Though the vicar married an English lady of good family, their son inherited his father's colour and features with all the prejudice that goes therewith, even (as the vicar sadly discovered) in 'Christian England'. True his ministry had won him respect over many years, but how could he continue that calling in the face of such a travesty of justice and, indeed, of a challenge to faith?

While their son was in custody awaiting trial, yet another animal was cruelly slashed. This, surely, the vicar cried jubilantly, proved their son's innocence! But the police were obdurate – George, they said, could be the leader of a gang who had perpetrated this latest outrage to get him off the hook. The vicar was astounded. Anybody less likely than George to lead a gang of violent men he could not imagine! George was

71

a shy, studious lad who never made friends easily. Also he had an alibi, vouched for by a respectable local trader, which covered the estimated time of the crime with which he was now charged. No matter, said Inspector Campbell, the prosecution now decided that the crime could have been committed several hours later, say, about 2 o'clock in the morning! 'George was sleeping in his bed,' averred the vicar who was sharing the room at the time. It was all to no avail. George was found guilty, on the flimsiest evidence imaginable, and sentenced to seven years.

Now, just three years later, he was homeward bound. What were his emotions as the train passed within a few feet of his vicarage home? There he would find not only the family who suffered with him, but possibly the reason behind this sudden freedom. Was the nightmare over at last? Had truth prevailed?

He was to find that it was a mystery to everyone. Yes, he was discharged from prison, but still under the surveillance of the police. No, he had not been cleared. So why had he been released? There were no satisfactory answers but he was to learn that during the past three traumatic years efforts had not flagged on his behalf. Lawyers who knew and trusted him had been appalled at this judicial farce and a petition to the Home Office had been signed by not less than 10,000 people.

But to no avail, or so it seemed. However, Mr R D Yelverton, an ex-Chief Justice of the Bahamas, had again taken up the case. George was still a convicted felon, struck off the roll of solicitors. What was he to do? Who could unravel the tangled tale? In a seemingly hopeless cul-de-sac, George himself had a bright idea. His lighter reading included the adventures of Sherlock Holmes. If only . . . but Sherlock was a fictional character. No matter – his creator, Sir Arthur Conan Doyle, was a man of flesh and blood. Sherlock was his brain child. And acting on a crazy impulse George Edalji appealed to the famous author. To Conan Doyle's credit although recovering from a bereavement and recent illness he was ready to put aside his influential friends, his enjoyment of travel, and his writing career to study the case of this victim of apparent injustice.

He scrutinised press cuttings, became convinced of Edalji's innocence and incensed at the dilemma the law now placed him in. It was obvious the authorities had serious doubts about the case but would go no further to rectify it. Meeting Edalji, he noticed at once that the young man's eyesight was so poor that he could not possibly have carried out the knife attacks with the necessary butcher's skill. Had nobody checked that? No, said Edalji, he himself had asked for an optician to be admitted as a witness; nobody had taken the slightest notice.

This was the first of many points raised by the author and published by *The Daily Telegraph* in a series running into 18,000 words! Soon the attention of the great British public was focussed on the Black Country village of Great Wyrley and Edalji's trial was exposed as the farce it must have been. The public was stirred. Letters flew back and forth and the Home Secretary promised a full investigation. That accomplished, 'Sherlock Holmes' put on his imaginary deerstalker and set out to track down the guilty party. Astonishingly for a man who was seldom in the Black Country and who lived many miles from the scene of the crimes, he came up with the identity of two brothers whose background and reputations fitted uncannily with his own mental assessment of likely culprits. During his investigation Sir Arthur received malevolent poison pen letters himself. Threats to relieve him of his own kidneys and liver (among other personal assets) proved him to be on the right track. A school failure turned butcher's apprentice, persecution of headmaster, racial hatred, handwriting identification, and a partner in crime, with the names of both, were part of corroborative evidence handed to the Home Office. No action was taken! Only the outbreak of the first World War ended those malicious antics.

However, thousands were delighted when Sir Arthur's painstaking eight month enquiry won for George Edalji a pardon, exonerating him completely from the crime for which he had been sentenced, and enabling lawyers to restore his name immediately to the solicitors' Roll. It is sad to admit that the Home Office, on a flimsy excuse, stopped short of awarding financial compensation. They had the gall to say that Edalji had not been cleared of writing the poison pen letters and so might have brought his trouble on himself! He had not, in fact, been tried on that charge! But the newspaper which featured his story invited subscriptions for him and the sum of £300 was raised. Also, history was made. From that time on legislation was launched to establish Courts of Criminal Appeal.

One further demonstration of Sir Arthur Conan Doyle's generous championship was yet to come. The marriage in September 1907 of Sir Arthur to Miss Jean Leckie was a glittering occasion with 250 guests present at the Hotel Metropole. Many famous writers and other celebrities graced the occasion and made a point of warmly welcoming a fellow guest – the young solicitor, George Edalji.

The Bespoke Coffin

A S an after dinner 'entertainment', a conducted tour of the greenhouse to view the host's own coffin may not have commended itself to all, even with the owner alive and hearty at his guest's side. But it is said that John Wilkinson rounded off many an evening's hospitality in this way, displaying the heavy iron casket for which he had been measured by his own ironworkers years before. He waxed eloquent about the advantages of iron over oak or elm for this important investment. Moreover, he would point out, an iron coffin was a distinct discouragement to body-snatchers. And there he had a point with which few would have disagreed.

Wilkinson was nothing if not generous in convivial company. In the greenhouse, alongside the bespoke coffin was a spare one which any guest might take free of cost providing the size was right. One might almost imagine him running a speculative eye over the assembled company. Alternatively, he would assure them, it would be no trouble to order a copy there and then, made to measure.

This looks like an early attempt at party selling, but in 1778 the host was 50 years old and a very successful businessman of many years standing. He had no need to tout for custom. His enthusiasm sprang from a longstanding love affair with iron ore. It had earned him a substantial fortune along with the nickname of 'Iron Mad' Wilkinson.

Perhaps it was his unceremonious arrival in the world which

launched him as an entrepreneur. He was born in a horse-drawn cart while his mother was returning from her market stall in Lindale, Cumbria. When in his 20s he moved south to Wolverhampton, then to Bilston to find employment in the mining industry. Within a few years he had his own business at Bradley with works in the villages of Linley and Willey also.

Wilkinson's inventive genius came to light with the building of the first blast furnace to use common coal in place of charcoal for smelting ore. This saved the felling of valuable trees for fuel, at a time when timber stocks had become almost irreplaceable and troubles abroad prevented timber from being imported. From then on the ironmaster progressed by leaps and bounds. The range of products which he fashioned from iron was a constant source of delight to himself and astonished other businessmen, apart from the practical rewards he reaped.

These were years of great opportunity in the Midlands. Wilkinson co-operated with Matthew Boulton, James Watt, Thomas Telford and the Darby family on several pioneering projects, the most notable being the first iron bridge between Broseley and Madeley. Some time later he was almost laughed to scorn, when he proposed to build an iron barge to sail on the Severn. But it came off, as did so many of his daring innovations. Onlookers stared in disbelief when the barge actually floated on the river at Willey.

It is said that everybody is entitled to make one mistake. John Wilkinson's came through investment in a waterworks enterprise in France in 1785. When our Continental neighbours rose in revolution and threw their country into chaos and terror, the ironmaster lost thousands of pounds through a business project in Paris. He was never paid for 40 miles of iron tubing laid to carry water under that great city and its environs. Disillusioned, he came back to concentrate on works in Staffordshire and over the Shropshire border.

For several years Wilkinson made his home at Broseley in Shropshire, at a point where he could stand on his doorstep at night and look toward the fiery sky over his Staffordshire furnaces. So sensitive was he to temperature and atmosphere in the foundries that he could tell whether the glow in the sky 'looked right'. And if he were not satisfied, whatever the time or the weather he would saddle his horse and ride over to investigate.

He is on record as a despot and a hard taskmaster, but he was highly respected by his workers, as witness this extract from a tribute composed in 1888, included in Jon Raven's *Urban and Industrial Songs of the Black Country and Birmingham.*

> 'You workmen of Bilston and Bradley draw near
> Sit down, take your pipes and my song you shall hear,
> I sing not of war or the state of the nation,
> Such subjects as these produce nought but vexation.
>
> 'But before I proceed any more with my tale,
> You shall all drink my health in a bumper of ale.
> Fill it up, and without any further parade
> John Wilkinson, boys, that supporter of trade!'

The ironmaster lived to the age of 80, dying at Castlehead, a mansion near his birthplace, Lindale. But despite his careful planning his burial became a tragi-comedy. He had outgrown his coffin. Even he, a mastermind with iron, had not made it expandable! Temporary interment in the garden at Castlehead had to suffice while another iron casket was made. When it arrived his body was re-interred in the plot he had himself selected, with a suitably inscribed iron monument set over it. The family then watched in trepidation as the whole thing sank lower and lower under the weight! Despite the prodigious effort it had to be re-interred in another plot in the garden which had a rock base. R.I.P.? Not quite.

In 1828 the Castlehead mansion was sold. The new owners were not happy at sharing the garden with the late owner. Resolutely they accomplished the task of lifting and conveying the casket and monument to the nearby churchyard. The authorities were resigned to accepting the coffin but drew the line at the iron monument and refused it entry. It rested forlornly at the roadside for some years before disappearing from the local scene.

Unfortunately this was not the only miscalculation the departed ironmaster made. After his wife died childless he had set up an alliance with another woman, resulting in three children being born without the benefit of marriage. His Will acknowledged this family as his beneficiaries, but made provision for a nephew in the event of their deaths. However, the nephew was not content to wait his turn and disputed the family's right on the grounds of illegitimacy. A seven year legal battle gave the nephew a short lived victory, but an appeal to the House of Lords finally swallowed up the ironmaster's fortune!

Wilkinson's real monument has to rest finally on his longstanding reputation as one of the chief builders of the county's prosperity in the Industrial Revolution.

The Princess Who Became A King

HOPE rides high in the heart of a child, and the boy and girl who looked on as their parents celebrated the signing of the Treaty of Wedmore in AD 878 might have envisaged Utopia ahead. Young Edward and Ethelfleda were the children of King Alfred the Great, and had been born and reared in a kingdom torn by Danish invasion, recurring conflict and endless privations. For far too long the Danes had occupied much of the kingdom of Mercia which included what we now know as Staffordshire, harassing the English, preventing the king from ruling his people in peace and carrying out the many reforms and benefits he longed to bring into national life. Now King Alfred had scored a spectacular victory, surrounding the Danes and imposing this treaty upon them as a condition of the truce.

This was King Alfred's greatest success to date and no one could have felt greater pride in him than his son and daughter. The treaty held out the best prospect of peace for years. Moreover Guthrum, the Danish leader, not only acknowledged defeat, but went on to embrace Christianity, with Alfred as his sponsor at the ceremony of baptism! This sign of grace was doubly welcome after Guthrum's past record, particularly in his barbaric treatment of humiliating, torturing and killing Edmund, the neighbouring King of the East Angles.

After the solemn ceremony the Danish leader kept his pledge to depart from Mercia, moving his forces back to where a line of demarcation had been agreed. Guthrum's leavetaking was amicable and the two great commanders parted with gifts and mutual goodwill. Now Alfred could settle to his administration. As a precaution, he set up the first English navy to meet future onslaughts at sea, and hopefully to keep the enemy off British soil as far as was humanly possible.

The king was singularly blessed in his loving, supportive family. He had married at the age of 20 a noble Mercian lady named Mercill, the mother of Edward and Ethelfleda. Their pride in him would have been enhanced as victories and diplomacy gradually brought other British kingdoms under his rule. Alfred had been a keen scholar since boyhood, and his children must have benefited from their father's love of learning and his pleasure in sharing it with others. Now they watched the king eagerly translating the works of Latin writers into the homely English language of his subjects.

Family life and King Alfred's working day were controlled by methodical timekeeping. He measured the 24 hours of each day by burning six wax candles in succession, each carefully designed to last four hours. As they grew to adult life the children witnessed his reforms in the realm of law and justice, and perhaps envied the ambassadors he sent overseas in search of greater and wider knowledge of the outside world.

Sadly, the navy could not for ever keep enemies from inland Britain. Succeeding Danish leaders refused to recognise Guthrum's treaty and thrust their way into Mercia yet again. But now Alfred's children were ready and willing to take their place in the field of conflict. A strong alliance resulted from the marriage of the king's daughter, Ethelfleda, to the ealdorman Ethelred, the acknowledged leader of the west Mercians, who now took the lead in defence.

Alfred's life came to an end at the turn of the century in AD 901. Nine years later the king's son, Edward, led a spectacular campaign against the enemy over a period of several weeks, defeating them in the Battles of Tettenhall, Womborne and Wednesfield. He may have lost his life in the conflict for we hear no more of him. It is the king's daughter, Ethelfleda, whose name has gone down into history as her father's worthy successor. Her marriage may have been an arranged one, to strengthen the position of her father, but it created a marvellous partnership between a couple united in a common cause.

It was a struggle which was to last 30 years. Ten years after losing her father, Ethelfleda became a widow but took command, soon to win acclaim as the illustrious daughter of a great king. 'Setting aside her domestic role,' says an old historian primly, 'Ethelfleda gave herself up entirely to the defence of her country.' For the next eight years she ruled the Mercians in her own right and was acclaimed King of Mercia!

Not only was she distinguished for her fighting prowess, but knowledge and wisdom acquired in childhood brought her recognition as a military engineer. She restored or rebuilt castles of strategic importance at Wednesbury and Stafford. The year AD 913 was of special significance. She arrived in Tamworth in early summer and built a fortress, part of which still survives. Tamworth then became her main home and the town acquired renewed importance.

Before his death, King Alfred had committed to his daughter the upbringing and education of her nephew, Athelstan. His early years were spent at Tamworth, and in the final brilliant achievements of her life Ethelfleda may well have been supported by him. Her death in AD 918 was greatly lamented. In course of time, when historians assessed her role, much credit for laying the foundation of a greater and wider kingdom was given to Ethelfleda.

Perhaps one of her finest accomplishments was that with it all she still retained the love of her people.

The Swan and
The Ugly Duckling

IT has to be said that the new doctor who arrived to make his mark in Lichfield in the mid 18th century was not a handsome man. Apart from his considerable bulk and careless attire, Erasmus Darwin's face was badly pox scarred. But, surprisingly, he attracted the opposite sex. He had a beautiful wife who was to bear him three sons, yet a number of women, including a charming girl in the literary circle at the Bishop's Palace, were fascinated by him.

Anna was the daughter of Canon Seward and was something of a hostess to the artistic circle because their venue, the Palace, was her father's home. Anna was intelligent and a gifted writer. Her grace and beauty earned for her the title 'the Swan of Lichfield'. To the doctor she may only have been a lighthearted digression whose company he enjoyed, and probably encouraged. Fascinated by him in her youth, she was to become his bitterest critic, waiting in the wings.

In pre-radio and television days a witty and lively conversationalist was worth his weight in gold – which, if true, set a very high value indeed upon the person of Dr Darwin. He was a big man, well over 6 ft tall, and in adult life weighed around 20 stones. But his personality was such that his company was eagerly sought. Despite a slight stammer he could hold an audience enthralled by his range of knowledge, his diversity of interests and the wit that never deserted him throughout his 71 years. He was still in his 20s when he established his practice at Lichfield and, though absorbed in many subjects outside his profession, was a very successful doctor. In particular he became widely known for his skill in diagnosis. His fame spread as far as the Capital where King George III and Queen Charlotte took note of him. They hoped he would move to London to become the king's physician. But Darwin was quite content with his life in Staffordshire, with his growing family and with the circle of friends around him. His personality made him a leading light in the literary and social group at the Palace. He loved the company of writers and poets, but postponed his own publishing ambitions at that time in case it. should impair his reputation as a serious medical man.

Bowling along the Staffordshire countryside Erasmus became a familiar figure. On foot he carried his bulky frame awkwardly following a knee injury resulting in permanent stiffness. This had been caused by a fall from his yellow chaise – all the harder to bear, perhaps, because the vehicle was designed by himself! It was known as a sulky; it held only one person. The doctor had to wedge himself in it. Fitted into the chaise was a bookshelf, some writing materials and a little store of confectionery to sustain Erasmus on his journey. Trotting behind the sulky came his horse, rather curiously named Doctor, saddled to carry his master when weather and road conditions put the sulky at a disadvantage.

For Erasmus it was a full and satisfying life, but his engrossment in it may have blinded him to dangers on the home front. Mary Darwin, always highly strung and temperamental, became ill, dosing herself secretly and rather unwisely. Then when only 31 years old, she died of alcoholism and liver disease in 1769.

Erasmus continued a longstanding association with a Mrs Parker who had run his household for some time – and given him two daughters to join the three sons born to Mary. For the moment that was all the romance he needed. He was much more absorbed in scientific matters with a growing circle of likeminded friends with whom he now associated on a regular basis. He developed a passion for designing inventions and was never offput by failures. 'A fool,' he reportedly said, 'is one who never tried an experiment.'

Darwin designed a windmill for the now famous Wedgwood pottery business, and then worked on a remarkable 'speaking tube' by which to communicate with occupants of other rooms. The story goes that he was so successful that an unsuspecting errand boy, warming himself by the kitchen fire, was petrified to hear a voice from the blaze demanding 'Bring me more coals'! When the use returned to his limbs the lad fled, never to enter the doctor's house again!

Then suddenly, nine years after his wife's death, the doctor's world was darkened by tragedy. Of the three sons born to him and Mary, Charles, the firstborn and favourite, had been despatched to Edinburgh to study medicine. But in the closing period of his studies he had the terrible misfortune to cut his finger while dissecting a child's brain. The cut turned septic. Erasmus was notified. He sped up to Edinburgh to join those trying to save 20 year old Charles. But in vain. Erasmus was devastated.

Some weeks later he came to terms with the loss and transferred his hopes and ambitions to his third son, 12 year old Robert, bypassing the elder surviving son who was his own namesake, and who was of a sombre and withdrawn nature, seemingly inherited from his mother. But Robert, like his father, was big and of a stronger, more outgoing personality. Medicine would not have been Robert's career by choice, but he made no demur as his father mapped out that course for him.

Two years later the 49 year old widower found further consolation when he married a widowed patient, 15 years his junior. Elizabeth Chandos-Pole and her two small daughters joined the household. It was astonishing that Erasmus could win this lady, for the years had not improved him. By now he was so gross that a semicircle was cut out of his place in the dining table to accommodate his bulk during meals! It took Elizabeth Darwin two years to accomplish her desire to get the family (including the new baby, Violetta) away from Lichfield and over to Derby.

Derby was only 25 miles from Lichfield, and though the circle of Erasmus's friends was shrinking as the years advanced, he continued to be part of the literary scene and of the scientific group known as the Lunar Society, meeting in Birmingham and Lichfield. In 1789 those two interests merged when the Society published his poem *The Loves of the Plants*. The title alone reveals the 'strong family trait which was to emerge more publicly 40 years hence through his grandson, Charles Darwin, and the voyage of the *Beagle*.

In the 13 years that remained to him the event which probably gave Erasmus most pleasure was the marriage of his son, Robert, by then a fully fledged doctor, to Susannah Wedgwood. She was the eldest and favourite daughter of his close friend, Josiah. The bride seems to have struck a harmonious note with Erasmus, travelling to Derby over a period of two years to give him piano lessons! It would have been his delight, too, to watch the professional success of Robert and his growing family, of which Charles, the future naturalist, was Robert and Susannah's fifth child.

Robert must have well fulfilled his father's hopes for him. He, too, was travelling country roads to reach patients in a bright yellow chaise, though in rather more style than his father had done. Robert boasted two handsome black horses and a splendidly apparelled coachman whose duties required him to dismount when arriving outside the homes of the poor and make a preliminary inspection to ensure that their floorboards and staircases could bear Dr Robert's 300 lbs weight! One wonders what transpired when the coachman brought an adverse report!

Erasmus's bachelor son (and namesake) never shook off the melancholy seemingly inherited from his mother. He had been trained to practise law but never did so. He was well provided for, but his father had watched, with some exasperation, this son's indecisiveness and irrational behaviour. He described it as 'a defect of voluntary power' – which sounds very much like the familiar 'needing to pull one's self together'.

When almost 40 years old, Erasmus Jnr left home during a heavy thunderstorm shortly after Christmas 1799, walked out into the river Derwent, and drowned. Erasmus Snr was nearing 70 at the time and was deeply shocked as he tackled the winding up of his son's estate. The son's affairs were in a hopeless muddle. It took the best part of the old doctor's last two years to accomplish the task. In April 1802 he moved from Derby into his son's house with Elizabeth and the remaining members of their family.

Two weeks later, on what seemed a normal Sunday morning, Erasmus arose before his family. After settling some altercation with a groom, he was writing a letter when suddenly overtaken by a shivering fit. Elizabeth and Violetta hurried down at a servant's summons, moved him to the fireside, and before his physician could arrive Erasmus Darwin's life flickered out. It was, Robert consoled the widow, exactly as he had wished – with the minimum of pain and fuss, and he helped Elizabeth to cope with the tributes that flowed in at the death of so prominent a Staffordshire personality and innovator.

But two years later came a bombshell when a scathing biography *The Life of Dr Darwin* was published by Anna Seward, that former 'Swan of Lichfield' who had been so enamoured of Erasmus all those years ago. Robert and his stepmother were incensed by it. Among other charges Anna claimed that Erasmus had been uncaring for the son who took his own life, and had called him 'a poor insane coward'! Robert was devastated as he strove to defend his father from what was virtually a character assassination.

In their fascinating family study *The Wedgwood Circle* (which includes material on Robert Darwin because he was married to Susannah) Barbara and Hensleigh Wedgwood reveal the extent of Robert's grief at this outcome: 'The image of his father as gross, coarse and cruel was as painful to him as the actual loss of his father.'

Anna Seward's vilification of the man who had once fascinated her seems a classic case of 'Hell hath no fury like a woman scorned'. Now she described him with relish as 'that large mass of genius and sarcasm'!

Robert accused Anna of inaccuracies, thwarted love and

revenge. He demanded a withdrawal. Only by threatening retaliation – to publish papers of his father's which would embarrass Anna – did Robert obtain a partial retraction. It seems that he then yielded to the persuasion of friends to draw a veil over the whole sad business. Unfortunately, say the Hensleigh Wedgwoods, the damage had been done. It is regrettably true that bad news not only travels fastest but lingers longest in the public's mind.

A Misfit
in Vanity Fair

EVEN before the sweeping success of Methodist revival
meetings in the Potteries and the Black Country there
appeared a profusion of old time biblical names in Staffordshire
parish registers in the 19th century. When the children of that
era grew to parenthood they, naturally, passed on their names,
thus Jobs, Calebs, Cyruses, and Isaiahs have abounded to this
day and make Staffordshire something of a 'Bible belt'.

Not all of the Staffordshire lads rejoiced in those biblical
names however. The eldest son and namesake of Enoch Bennett
from the shabby corner shop at No. 90 Hope Street in Hanley
declined, as soon as he was old enough, to go through life
named after an unworldly patriarch who walked humbly but
closely with his God. Enoch Arnold Bennett, born in 1867 into
an impoverished home, developed a taste for the good life in
a more material sense. Using his second name he was to bring
fame to himself and to the Potteries by his graphic portrayal
of life there.

All of this he achieved from a background of childhood
poverty and denial. Eight brothers and sisters joined him in
that deprived household, to lay claim to the resources of a father
who was manfully struggling to better himself. Enoch Snr
deserves the utmost credit for climbing out of his humble pottery
job by coping with law studies even while providing for the
needs of that ever growing household. By the time he was 31
years old Enoch Snr had qualified as a solicitor, opened his own

practice, and moved his big brood to 205 Waterloo Road, Burslem.

So it is not surprising that when Enoch Jnr did well enough at his Newcastle-under-Lyme school to qualify for a place at Cambridge University, he was denied that chance and obliged instead to join the law practice in Burslem. Self help was the order of the day in the Bennett domain. However, Enoch the son never fully appreciated the security of a career in law. He found his whole situation and surroundings uncongenial. His personality and temperament clashed with his father's, and he was depressed by the soulless, smoke-belching ovens and chimneys dominating the local scene. Vision and ambition struggled within him distracting him from dusty parchments and dry legal jargon. Then shorthand classes in the Wedgwood Institute opened up a new outlet for him. By the time he was 21 years old London's Lincoln's Inn Fields beckoned him to a wider sphere, first with a legal firm offering 4 sovereigns a week.

Here Arnold Bennett, as he was now known, had the good fortune to encounter an artistic friend who took him under his own roof in Chelsea and introduced him to a lively, artistic circle. Soon a prizewinning entry in a *Tit-Bits* competition launched him into a journalistic career on that paper. Now the self confidence and brashness which had been discouraged in Burslem stood him in good stead. Financial prospects spurred him on to secure the assistant editorship of the weekly magazine *Woman*. By now his father in Burslem had mustered sufficient faith in his son's enterprise to provide the £300 investment money required.

Short stories and articles flowed from Arnold Bennett's pen, and soon after his 30th birthday came the publication of his first novel *The Man from The North*. Though not a money spinner (it earned him a profit of only £1) it brought friendship and encouragement from other writers, Joseph Conrad and H G Wells among them. Four years later, in 1902, the much more popular *Anna of the Five Towns* was published. This novel established the link between his undoubted talent, his ability to write clearly and understandably, and his keen observation of life in the Potteries. The industries, the workers, and the grim and grimy atmosphere of Tunstall, Burslem, Hanley, Longton and Stoke-on-Trent are clearly portrayed by names thinly disguised. The five towns (now regarded as districts of Stoke-on-Trent) straggled along an 8 mile winding road, the familiar haunts of his childood and adolescence.

But it was reviews, magazine articles and serial stories which brought Bennett the affluence desired since childhood. Then, somewhat bedazzled by Continental life and writers, the man from the Potteries entered a completely new sphere by moving to Paris. He found life there very agreeable and married in July 1907 a Parisian, Marguerite Soulie. He was then 40 years old and absorbed in his career, so the marriage was not tremendously important to him. Even so, the couple spent 14 years together there, during which he produced a vast amount of witty, humorous journalism and what became his greatest novel, *The Old Wives' Tale*. It became popular in America and established Bennett as a serious English novelist. A life of luxury in the company of the rich and famous was his reward.

He managed one more novel while living in Paris – *Clayhanger* – another graphic tale of life in the Potteries. But now he was paying the price of concentration. Eyestrain, neuralgia and insomnia brought him back to his native land with his capacity for high living and expensive tastes undiminished.

Bennett continued writing from a luxury flat in London and though apparently wallowing in self indulgence in the Capital and aboard his prized yacht, he surprised contemporaries in 1923 by coming up with a masterpiece. *Riceyman's Steps* featured two contrasting characters – a mean spirited secondhand bookseller and a girl who was virtually a drudge. It was an affecting tale, revealing the author's essential humanity. Bennett's last book, *Imperial Palace,* is said to mirror life in the Savoy Hotel, featuring scenes of luxury and glitter with which he was not unfamiliar. His life was nearing its end, so it is sad to note that this last work did not have a strong appeal to the public. He died in March 1931, just a year after its publication.

Almost every reviewer of the writer's life reproaches him for pandering to popular taste and easy money, instead of reserving his talent for the good literature of which he was capable. Arthur Mee, who himself wrote with almost loving dedication about 'the King's England', sadly concluded that Bennett's lifestyle and highly paid inferior work constituted a betrayal of talent and a suppression of his true humanity. He detected in Bennett a genuine compassion for his fellow men and was convinced that he was built for better things. He saw Bennett as 'a misfit in Vanity Fair'.

So, perhaps below that self indulgent surface the author had more in common with his patriarchal namesake than at first appeared.

Well Might
The Willow Weep

ALL through Saturday night and into the small hours of Sunday morning John Holdcroft's mother searched for her nine year old son and returned home to Commercial Street in Sneyd Green without finding the slightest clue to his whereabouts. He had left home early on that August morning of 1833 to walk to his work at the Burslem pottery of Joseph Hawley. It was a Saturday. Thanks to Lord Shaftesbury's reforms, children's work hours had just been limited to nine hours a day with a one and a half hour meal break. So John would have finished work at 7 o'clock that evening. Mrs Holdcroft did not expect him to come straight home. The long day's work in summer heat often tempted boys to stop off at Bycars Pool for a dip, or at least for a stroll, a game or some relaxation in the fields while daylight lasted. Despite the increasing industries in the area, it was still pleasantly rural between towns and villages.

As the evening wore into nightfall Mrs Holdcroft really did begin to worry. Saturday was pay day. Had John been persuaded to go with other boys to the races at Etruria? The village built by Josiah Wedgwood 50 years earlier was now a centre of recreation and various attractions, as well as of industry. Even so, John should have been home by nine or ten o'clock, surely? And what about his week's wages – 18 pence, which was slightly above normal for a boy of his age. Had he guarded it carefully? Was he afraid to come home because it was gone? True the Wakes Week had begun at Hanley – and who knows what ruffians were lurking around dark fair booths on a pay day – but would Johnnie have gone there? Surely not without saying something before he left home that morning. All these and a thousand more questions flooded into the mind of the now thoroughly anxious mother until she felt she must go out and make enquiries. Any activity was better than none.

Crossing Crabtree Field she found the area around the pool and nearby canal banks empty and silent by that time, giving no clue whatever, and also drew a blank on hammering at the factory door. When traced, the cashier could confirm that John had been in line to receive his wages that day alongside others, but no one remembered seeing the boy after he left at the usual time with other lads on that shift.

Who would have been with John when he left? The most likely fellow was 15 year old Charles Shaw, also of Sneyd Green. They must often have walked home together, and Mrs Holdcroft may have felt reassured that the slightly built younger boy had a bigger, more robust companion on the pay day walk home. She may not have thought much of the Shaw family, and the lad himself was pretty rough – but 'better the devil you know'.

So to the Shaw's home she went with her urgent enquiry. Had Charles come home from work? Oh, yes, he was fast asleep in bed. What was wrong? Roused from sleep Charles affirmed that he could shed no light on the little boy's disappearance, and went back to his bed selfishly unperturbed. Now Mrs Holdcroft had nowhere to turn, except home to await events.

For most folk the Sunday dawned bright and cheerful – it was the beginning of 'the Wakes' and high days and holidays were few and far between. They must make the most of it. But for Mrs Holdcroft it was the culmination of a nightmare. A neighbour walking his dog early in Crabtree Field was alerted by the animal's behaviour to sweep aside the soft green curtain of a willow tree's foliage and reveal a small, still form with a tell-tale cord around the neck! It was Johnnie Holdcroft.

Soon the police carried out the sad task of conveying the boy's body to the Etruria Inn and began their investigation. It did not take long to find a couple of boys who, while enjoying a swim in Bycars Pool on the previous day, had fallen foul of the quarrelsome Charlie Shaw. Yes, little John Holdcroft had been with him and had paid the penalty of being Shaw's companion when a fight ensued. It had been easier to punch the defenceless Johnnie in revenge for Shaw's attack, and blood had been drawn from his nose. What made this information so significant was that an adult stroller along the canal had later seen a small lad with a bloodstained nose being chased by a taller one gripping a cord as he ran.

It took very little time to establish that the cord used to strangle Johnnie before robbing him of his pitiful last wages, was a packer's cord from the Hawley pottery to which Charles Shaw had access. Shaw's own wages had been drastically cut that week through nobody's fault but his own. Coupled then with his bloodstained garment and matching footprints beneath the willow tree, it did not take long to make an arrest despite stout denials of guilt.

At Shaw's trial defence pleas of an inherited mental defect, possible brain damage from a fall, a bite from a mad dog and a kick from a horse all failed to move the jury. The accused remained callously indifferent throughout it all. When sentence of death (because of his age) was commuted to transportation, it may have been fortunate for Shaw. But much less promising for the unfortunates 'down under'!

Dictionary Johnson

SAMUEL Johnson was an extraordinary character. Stafford-shire is justly proud of him. Not only a great writer (some say *the* greatest) of the 18th century, but he was a sparkling conversationalist and dynamic personality. As compiler of the first comprehensive English dictionary we all owe him a great debt. How complacently we turn to the many available versions we have today, and never give a thought to the nine years of drudgery Johnson put into a work which stabilized the English language. Was it drudgery? It is thus described by some biographers. But Johnson read widely, and objectively, loved language and mulled over each syllable of a word almost with relish. He traced its origin, pinpointed its true meaning, added alternative uses, and even illustrated its meaning by pertinent quotations. In fact, it was something of an encyclopaedia and it established his literary fame.

What an exciting day it was when London booksellers recognised his skill with words and financed the whole project for £1,500 or thereabouts! It made them a profit but was not a great financial boost for Johnson considering the time taken and his outlay in employing others to copy passages and quotations; he even lodged some of them in his own home! It earned him the nickname of Dictionary Johnson, and led to the grant of a pension by the king which relieved him of the financial strain which had shadowed his earlier life.

Johnson's statue stands in the market square at Lichfield, opposite his birthplace at the bookshop of his father Michael Johnson. The hasty infant baptism on the very day of young Samuel's birth in September 1709 testifies to his precarious start in life. But despite scars from scrofula and poor eyesight, he survived and came through his schooldays with credit. Leaving Lichfield Grammar School, he spent a couple of years reading avidly while giving some rather desultory assistance in the bookshop. His elderly father was struggling to make ends meet by taking his wares to market stalls in nearby towns. Michael Johnson had commenced the bookshop in the square some 30 years before his son was born, and was established as a highly respected citizen holding a succession of important civic offices. But he was haunted by a lack of money through an unwise investment, an attempt to manufacture parchment – and this at a time when 20,000 debtors already languished in prison!

In later years Samuel Johnson wrote rather frankly about his home life being overcast by the lack of security and his father's recurring bouts of depression. It seems that his parents were not ideally suited in their rather late marriage. From his father Samuel inherited his big frame and his intellect, but he had a very real love and respect for his well born though less gifted mother. She once soothed his schoolboy apprehensions by saying 'We often come off best when we are most afraid.' School discipline was harsh in those days and Samuel made no secret of having been at the receiving end of it, clever pupil though he was.

When this son was in his early 20s the bookseller was generous enough to sacrifice a £40 legacy to send him to Oxford University. Samuel possessed a good stock of books and a fantastic memory for retaining all that he read. However, his happiness was still clouded by lack of money and he left university early without a degree to embark on a precarious attempt to maintain himself by writing and teaching.

Soon after this, in 1732, Samuel's father died and the family found their assets to be meagre indeed. Mrs Johnson (with a younger son about whom little is heard apart from his early death) continued the business. Three years later Samuel, after one or two brief excursions into romance, met and married a widow almost twice his age, Mrs Elizabeth Porter. He seems to have developed a sincere attachment to her, as well as to

Lucy Porter, a stepdaughter not much younger than himself. She went to live and work with Johnson's mother at the bookshop. It seems a general opinion that the new bridegroom was not an attractive man physically, by now heavily built, clumsy of dress and deportment, and not particularly well mannered. It was his mind which attracted Elizabeth Porter. After 15 minutes together she remarked 'This is the most sensible man I have ever met in my life.'

Together they opened a small boarding school in their home at Edial, near Lichfield, offering Latin and Greek languages. Pupils were so scanty that it closed and Samuel, in company with one young scholar, David Garrick, set out for London with only a few pence between them to seek fame and fortune. Eventually both achieved this after years of struggle in poor lodgings and cheap eating houses. For at least one night Johnson walked the streets when he could not afford a bed!

Garrick's theatrical connections brought better days. Johnson's first play *Irene* ran only briefly at Drury Lane Theatre but brought some recognition and enabled him to fetch his wife, familiarly known as Tetty, to join him in London. He wrote for *The Gentleman's Magazine* and other London periodicals, then developed his talent for verse with *London* and *The Vanity of Human Wishes*. In his mid 30s came the colossal undertaking which absorbed most of his working hours for the next nine years. The dictionary established his name though, sadly, first his wife and then his mother had died by the time it was fully acclaimed. He expressed his sorrow in verse.

The grant of a £300 a year pension by the young King George III did not occur until 1762. The sheer necessity of providing for his mother's funeral in 1759 drove Sam Johnson to rush through in one week his novel *Rasselas*. It opens with a revealing and nostalgic sentence:

'You who listen with credulity to the whispers of fancy, and peruse with eagerness the phantoms of hope; who expect that age will perform the promises of youth, and that the

99

deficiences of the present day will be supplied
by the morrow, attend to the history of
Rasselas, Prince of Abissinia.'

But happily his own 'phantoms of hope' materialised. His
pension afforded him relaxation and time to enjoy the company
of other men of letters and fame in homes and clubs. A frequent
companion appears to have been Sir Joshua Reynolds, but he
also developed new friendships – significantly that of James
Boswell. This young Scot, son of the Laird of Auchinleck, came
to London eagerly seeking acquaintance with artistic
contemporaries, and managed to court the attention of the now
famous Dr Samuel Johnson. (Trinity College, Dublin, had
given him his Doctorate and Oxford University conferred a
Master of Arts degree in 1765.)

Boswell admits to being momentarily offput by the now quite
pronounced muscular spasms which some strange malady had
brought upon Sam Johnson. To cope with this embarrassing
jerking and rolling movement of head and body, on top of his
earlier sicknesses (poor eyesight and a recurring melancholia
inherited from his father), was a triumph of determination and
due to the doctor's continuing eagerness for society and
converse. The awkward spasms ceased the moment he launched
into his usual lively talk and James Boswell was fascinated. So
began the epic friendship which eventually brought to us the
delightful, revealing biography *The Life of Samuel Johnson,* and
to Boswell himself lasting fame.

No other biography compares with Boswell's *Life* and his
Journal of a Tour to the Hebrides with Samuel Johnson. They are
packed with lively debate and surprising – even comic –
domestic scenes. In his home Johnson sheltered an incompatible
group of men and women who were refugees from misfortune.
They turned his kitchen into a battleground! Where did he find
peace to write?

Small wonder that he enjoyed the London clubs, one of which
he founded, where he could find the stimulation of
contemporary minds. His wit enlivened any debate. He

disagreed, for instance, that one should be tolerant toward a person who challenged one's cherished beliefs. 'Then we should pity such a man,' argued his opponent, to which Johnson retorted:

> 'Why, Sir to be sure when you wish a man to have that belief which you think is of infinite advantage, you wish well to him; but your primary consideration is your own quiet. If a madman were to come into this room with a stick in his hand, no doubt we should pity the state of his mind; but our primary consideration would be to take care of ourselves. We should knock him down first and pity him afterwards.'

Whenever he returned to Lichfield, Johnson was welcomed with delight by friends of his youth and by his stepdaughter. An inheritance enabled Lucy to build for herself a fine home in Tamworth Street where he often stayed. In 1776 he took Boswell to meet them all, and booked in at The Three Crowns, an old fashioned inn adjoining his old home. Together they entered on a round of visits. Invitations poured in to breakfasts, early dinners, afternoon teas and supper evenings. It was diverting to find Johnson taking tea with the clergyman's widow who had been his first love, and visiting the theatre, the venue of another romantic spell. 'Forty years ago', he confided to Boswell, 'I was in love with an actress here, Mrs Emmet, who played Flora in 'A Hob in the Well'.'

They attended the production of *Theodosius* by Stratford players in the Town Hall which served as a temporary theatre. Johnson took a seat in the pit and was lionized by many in the audience. There followed a supper with lively and enjoyable discourse at the Bishop's Palace in the company of the resident Canon Seward and his daughter, Anna, 'The Swan of Lichfield'.

Because the oats of his native Scotland had been derided as the 'food of horses' it pleased Boswell to find oat cakes on Lichfield tables – though lacking the crispness of Scottish ones! He was bemused, too, at the county dialect after Dr Johnson had championed the inhabitants of Lichfield as 'the most sober, decent people in England, the genteelest in proportion to their wealth, and spoke the purest English'! He smiled at the provincial slant. 'There', instead of rhyming with 'pair', rhymed,with 'fear'! And the word 'once' (normally like 'dunce') had the higher pitch in Staffordshire of 'woonse'.

All in all the friends had a delightful time and during a hallowed Sunday afternoon in the cathedral (both men stood firm in Christian belief) Boswell sat alongside Johnson and indulged in a little hero worship:

> 'It was grand and pleasing to contemplate this
> illustrious writer, now in full fame, worshipping
> in 'the solemn temple' of his native city.'

In July 1784 Lichfield's most illustrious son visited the city, conscious of failing health. He stayed much longer than usual, wrote many interesting and topical letters and shared memories with friends of his boyhood and youth. Naturally, his thoughts turned to the family whose mortal remains lay in the centre aisle of Saint Michael's church. A loving epitaph commemorated them all, and in particular honoured the father to whom he might have given more support when living in Lichfield.

Before leaving the city he confided to a clergyman friend the one day in particular which weighed upon his conscience:

> 'I refused to attend my father to Uttoxeter
> Market. Pride was the source of that refusal and
> the remembrance of it was painful. A few years
> ago I desired to atone for this fault. I went to
> Uttoxeter in very bad weather and stood for a
> considerable time bareheaded in the rain, on the
> spot where my father's stall used to stand. In
> contrition I stood, and I hope the penance was
> expiatory.'

This tale has given some lustre to Uttoxeter Market and may be an oft repeated one. But if so, it can only be because, at heart, all the world loves a penitent.

Dr Johnson returned to London and died about eight weeks after this touching admission, subsequently being buried with well deserved honours in Westminster Abbey.

Making
a Song and Dance

DESPITE their hardship and poverty, when fortunes
fluctuated in the Black Country, and even during times
of bitter industrial strife, workers were never slow to come up
with a song and dance to fit any and every occasion.

Mainly their songs were very simple, somewhat strident and
sometimes dominated by dialect not easily understood by alien
ears. Many songs must have been composed on the spur of the
moment in convivial company, spontaneously adding verse by
verse, for they often reached a considerable length. But what
mattered the imperfections or redundant syllables? Taken up
in the spirit of comradeship, such songs sustained the workers
in lean and hungry times and brought about a unity of purpose
that somehow spurred them on.

The Nailmakers' Strike, for instance, (written in 1862), after
a verse or two proclaiming their pitiful state, is a plea for Britain
to show charity at home.

> 'Oh the slaves abroad in the sugar canes,
> Find plenty to help and to pity their pains,
> But the slaves at home in the mine and fire,
> Find plenty to pity but none to admire.
>
> Oh I wish I could see all Nail Dealers,
> Draw such a load as did we poor Nailors,
> And to feel such punishment and such smart,
> That it may soften their hard, stony hearts.'

Sadly, their plea, for the most part, fell upon deaf ears.

Songs from coal workers are plentiful. *The Collier Lads Who Labour Underground* is a stout defence of their grimy, toilsome work and provides an eloquent reminder of their importance to the rest of the community, as these sample verses show:

'Come attend awhile you working men
  wherever you may be,
I pray you give attention and listen unto me,
It's concerning of poor collier lads,
  their equal ne'er was found,
For all trades are depending on
  the lads that are under ground.

The mariner where'er he steers across the raging sea,
Mechanics, too, and artizans with their machinery
Have all to thank the collier lad
  while danger did surround
So ne'er despise the gallant lads
  that labour under ground.'

In the early part of the 20th century *The Chainmakers' Song* was published in sheet form, and suggests that hard driven though he might be, the manual labourer found breath enough to provide his own 'music while you work':

As long as the smoke goes upward,
  so long will I love you, dear,
All day long 'mid the fact'rys din
  I'm longing to have you near,
I can see your face in the fire light, as long
  as I look at the glowing heat,
And the sound of each blow on the anvil
  seems to ring out your name so sweet.'

But sadly the weaver working in or around the same period, heard a more doleful message coming from his loom:

105

'Poverty, poverty knock!
Me loom is a-saying all day.
Poverty, poverty knock!
Gaffer's too skinny to pay.
Poverty, poverty knock,
Keepin' one eye on the clock.
Ah know ah can guttle
When ah hear me shuttle
Go: Poverty, poverty knock.'

Happily, gloom and doom did not prevail for ever. Staffordians rallied smartly to commemorate special events. For instance it was an exciting day for Wolverhampton in the early part of the 19th century when an unidentified object was seen in the sky approaching the town. It was well worth celebrating in song.

'When the balloon flew o'er 'Ampton Town
The Wofflers they did staer.
They thowt it was a coal boat
A'flying through the aer,
So trew it is un-to the time
So trew it is I o-wun
Going to fetch a load of lime
To build a sun and mewn.'

Balloon ascents were very rare in those days, and it appears the intrepid traveller was a Mr Sadler from nearby Birmingham. 'The Wofflers' incidentally were merely onlookers in our less picturesque language.

History becomes more comprehensible to many of us when isolated incidents are recounted in song. Whether the tale of the encounter between the tanner of Tamworth and King Edward IV is based on fact or not, it emerges as a lengthy ballad, well documented from 1596 onward, and achieves some authenticity by being included in Bishop Percy's *Reliques*. A shorter version (only 23 verses long!) is the most popular one.

The scene is thought to be set on the Tamworth road, near Basset's Pole.

Now that the long, tortuous Wars of the Roses are over, with tall, handsome Edward of York on the throne, the country is beginning to resume its role as Merrie England. The king has a mischievous impulse to conceal his identity, dismiss his companions into hiding, and make sport of his humble subjects. He sets out to hunt at Drayton Basset just as a tanner is returning from a Birmingham market. The king hails the tanner by asking the way to Drayton Basset and is told:

> 'To Drayton Basset woldst thou goe,
>> Fro' the place where thou does stand
> The next payre of gallows thou comest unto,
>> Turn in upon thy right hand.
>
> "That is an unready waye," said our King.
>> "Thou doest but jest, I see:
> Now shewe me out the nearest waye,
>> And I pray thee wend with mee." '

This the tanner declines, even when offered payment and is convinced in his own mind that this well dressed adventurer is none other than a gentleman highway robber of whom there were plenty roaming the roads in those days.

However, the man is tempted, by a splendid offer of gold, to exchange horses, though flatly refusing to sell his stock in trade, the cowhide.

> ' "But if so be we needs must change,
>> As change thou must abide,
> Though thou has gotten Brock, my mare,
>> Thou shalt not have my cow-hide."
>
> The tanner took the good cow-hide
>> That of the cow was hilt,
> And threw it upon the king's saddle
>> That was so fairly gilt.

But when the steed saw the cow-tail wag,
      And eke the black cow-horn,
The steed began to run away,
      As the devil the tanner had borne.

The tanner he pulled, the tanner he sweat
      And held by the pummell fast;
At length the tanner came tumbling downe:
      His neck he had well-nigh brast.'

The injured tanner pleads for his mare's return and is at his wits end when the 'highwayman' demands a high price. But the king's sense of humour being now satisfied, he blows his bugle, calls his attendants and the truth is revealed to the now terrified tanner.

The prank ends happily enough with the king making the astonished tanner a magnificent gift of the manor and lands of Plumpton Park, and grateful thanks conclude the happy-ever-after tale.

What better way to celebrate highdays and holidays than with Morris Dances? In the 1800s Lichfield teams, in particular, danced with exceptional vigour and dexterity on Whit Mondays. Their teams numbered eight to a group, instead of the usual six, and with gaily adorned smocks, flying ribbons, clashing staffs and tinkling bells, they made it a day to remember.

But most spectacular of Staffordshire celebrations must surely be the Horn Dance of Abbots Bromley. It originated in the distant past, some claim as early as the 12th century, yet still provides the principal entertainment on the first Monday in Wakes Week. A dozen men take part, half of them form the dance team, each lowering on to his shoulders a pair of reindeer antlers mounted on carved wooden deerheads. The top of the spiky horns extend well above the dancer's head and project in front of his face. A short pole attached to the quite heavy contraption provides a steadying grip by the wearer's left hand during the vigorous dance movement.

Half of the dancers wear white painted horns and the rest

are painted blue. The other six performers (all male) are also in costume – a jester, a musician, a hobby horse, a 'Maid Marion', a boy bowman and a second lad carrying a triangle. Inevitably some changes in movement, instruments, rhythm and more colourful dress have crept in over the centuries. 'Maid Marion' wears a flowing white veil with ankle-length dress, and carries a wooden ladle in which to collect coins for charities. The dancers wear flat caps, sleeveless jerkins and knee breeches in colour schemes of red, gold, green and brown with knitted green stockings.

Basically this remains the traditional, vigorous, entertainment handed down through the ages. The dancers commence by forming a circle, the leader breaking out to form a loop until the six become two lines of three, advancing upon each other in a pretended charge. The antlers come into play as they raise them to feign a locking movement before passing through the opposite rank to re-form the circle and repeat the sequence. The music, the beating of the triangle and the rhythmic clacking of the hobby horse's jaws add animation to the lively, colourful performance.

The team fills the day with repeat performances, following their chosen leader who pays for his prestige by bearing the heaviest pair of antlers, weighing over 25 pounds! Then back to base for a final performance in the village street before returning the 'props' to the local church. Here they repose for twelve months until called upon again to take pride of place in preserving what must be the county's oldest and liveliest custom.

Foiled
by a Donkey

A S if it were not trauma enough to part with the earthly remains of someone loved and lost, mourners in some parts of England in the 18th century suffered the added dread of having the grave despoiled by body snatchers. After dark it was possible for heartless, ghoulish robbers to return with all stealth, when no living soul would be in the churchyard, to dig away the newly turned earth, lift the coffin to the surface, remove the body and cart it away, usually to sell for medical research or student instruction. These robbers had the gall to call themselves 'resurrection men' and the only way to be sure of defeating the cruel desecration was to mount a heartbreaking vigil over the newly filled grave for two or three nights. After this the danger passed because the body could no longer serve its grim purpose.

It so happens that the Potteries had not suffered much from these ghoulish marauders, perhaps because there were no adjacent teaching hospitals. Then a couple of strangers moved into a near derelict cottage, renovated it and invested in a horse and unusually long, narrow cart. Not pottery men as almost all local inhabitants were, so they must be setting up in business, neighbours conjectured, but found the newcomers rather uncommunicative as to its nature.

And apparently with good reason, for on a dark and stormy night the two men ventured forth to visit the village church at Bucknall.

It so happened that the road ran closely alongside the wall of the churchyard, and somewhere near midnight the couple stealthily entered with horse and cart through the small gate. A few yards inside they tethered the animal to a convenient railing and moved across to locate the wanted grave. It was a wild and blustery night. No one would be abroad at such a time. Potbank workers retired early for work next morning. All was silent as the grave. They set to work with pickaxe and spades.

But moving along the road adjoining the graveyard, swiftly as wind and darkness would allow, came one Sauntering Ned, a 30 year old potman-turned-pedlar. He had enjoyed a good day at Cheadle market with his pottery wares and was returning to the dilapidated thatched cottage on the edge of the village which was his bachelor domain. Ned knew the Potteries well, having been born into a potting family going back several generations. But he was a man of the open air, a lover of the green turf, shady trees in summer, plants, flowers and the sound of birdsong. It was claustrophobic for him to be shut up for many hours of the day at a workman's bench, and he had opted out of his trade. Old Toft, his boss, had supplied him with a few cheap pots from his stock of black ware and set him on the road to enterprise in 1797 with a small hawker's basket.

It took courage in those days to go out on the open road knowing thieves and vagabonds would lie in wait for a returning salesman with his day's takings. But Ned was no fool. Old fashioned and shabby in appearance, he had a ready wit, knew how to handle business, and had the sense to take precautions. As soon as he could afford it he bought a donkey, knocked up a makeshift stable alongside the cottage and enjoyed the animal's companionship and co-operation with the loads. As a means of protection (especially on night journeys) he fastened a metal chain to the donkey's hind leg, creating an unearthly sound to offput prowlers. At likely danger points he slipped a peculiar horned head-dress over its pointed ears.

Arrayed thus, at the slightest alarm, Ned could charge down the road to frighten off a threatened ambush. The tracks were rough and narrow, hedged about with thick concealing bushes and undergrowth. Many a time Ned was glad of his precautions, and he was to put them to good use on that wild and windy night in 1797 on his way back from Cheadle market.

As the donkey neared the graveyard gate, a few feet ahead of its master, it stopped, listened, turned in and encountered the horse tethered inside. With Ned bemusedly following, the donkey wandered on. Locating sounds at the open grave it lumbered curiously over the intervening mounds, its chain rattling and clanging on adjacent stones. The diggers – down inside the opened grave – paused in utter consternation. Just as the donkey reached them, one man ventured to stand and peep over the graveside. The horned and hooded donkey stared down over the edge! The intruders were petrified. Then with a yell of 'My God, Jim, the Devil!', the first man scrambled up the opposite side of the grave and sped away with his companion panting after him.

The two were never seen again. The cottage which they had taken was left empty. As for the horse and cart, what better than for Ned, who had thoughtfully filled in the desecrated grave, to take home a new companion along with his donkey, and set up an even more prosperous business forthwith.

The
King's Protector

'For the next week she carried the crown of England in her hands and never was trust more bravely or delicately performed.'

STAFFORDSHIRE will always be proud of Jane Lane. Sir Arthur Bryant's warmhearted appraisal sums up the magnitude of the part she played in restoring the monarchy. Three days after his defeat at Worcester, 21 year old Charles II crossed into Staffordshire at dead of night. He dismounted and hobbled painfully, on tender feet, across a field which adjoined the road, to find a black-garbed figure waiting under a shadowed grove of trees in the far corner. Father Huddleston, the Catholic priest, quickly conducted His Majesty through a nearby gate and across the garden of Moseley Hall into the fine home of Mr Thomas Whitgreave.

With what emotion that household greeted the tall bedraggled fellow disguised with cropped hair and rough garb! Charles learned that already plans were in hand to take him onward in further flight. But first he must get to the panelled bedroom upstairs, have the mud and grit sponged from him and his poor feet bathed, get into a change of clothing and enjoy his first night's rest in a good bed since leaving the battlefield.

Next morning he enjoyed a breakfast with his host's mother and settled to take advantage of 36 hours respite amid the comforts of Moseley Hall. Much of Monday, the first day, he spent in a small room over the front porch, scanning the main road beyond the front gate and catching up with what scanty news filtered through of other escapees. At nightfall he was happily reunited with a Royalist officer, Lord Wilmot, who had ridden the few miles from Colonel Lane's home, Bentley Park, to outline a plan for the next stage in the king's escape. Throughout Tuesday Charles was more relaxed and Father Huddleston and the host enjoyed his company. They had a preview of the charm, wit, political awareness and philosophical outlook which would emerge in England in later years. They were treated also to some unexpectedly shrewd comments on randomly chosen portions from a Bible which lay at hand in the study.

At midnight Colonel Lane arrived with a spare horse to collect the king, who first exchanged farewells with Huddleston and the Whitgreaves – a touching display of homage on their part and a pledge of remembrance on the king's. Charles then left with the Colonel to ride for Bentley and to be disguised for his role in the next act of the drama. The king was to 'stand in' for William Jackson, Jane Lane's humble attendant (for whom she already possessed a travel permit) on a journey to Bristol. From there it was desperately hoped that Charles would find a ship and escape England's shores.

At dawn the horses were saddled and the 'servant' stood waiting for Mistress Jane and her cousin, Henry Lascelles, in the driveway. Charles mounted, Jane took her place behind him, and from that moment upon her frail shoulders fell the responsibility of taking her king to freedom. By midday Staffordshire was left behind for the three days' journey through Warwickshire and Gloucestershire with heart-stopping crises en route. To keep up the subterfuge, Jane had been obliged to speak roughly to her manservant, and once ventured to cuff his ears!

They reached Bristol at last and Jane entered upon the family business for which she had obtained the travel permits. But no boat was available for the king and Jane's ordeal was prolonged. She could not abandon her 'servant' in a household which,

115

largely, did not know his true identity. They would expect him to leave with her. In great secrecy an alternative escape route was taken, heading eastward through Dorset as if making for home in Staffordshire. They then returned south to reach Trent where Jane could safely relinquish her charge into the hands of Colonel Frank Wyndham. His past connections with the royal family ensured a welcome, and confidence was reinforced as he told them of the solemn deathbed injunction uttered by his late father, ending with '. . . honour and obey your sovereign, and though the crown should hang upon a bush, I charge you forsake it not!' Charles was in good hands.

Jane and her cousin Lascelles returned to Bentley in good heart. Their welcome was attended by great relief and rapt attention to their account of nailbiting encounters during the momentous week's journey. It was a week to be remembered – surely eclipsing anything that had occurred during 200 years of the Lanes' family history at Bentley Park.

In the course of time the secret leaked out and Jane's own liberty was at stake. She and the brother who had also connived in the escape were obliged to flee the country. Jane's royal 'serving man' met her on the Continent and gave her into the care of the Princess of Orange. When the happy day of the Restoration dawned, Jane was suitably rewarded by the sovereign who owed his survival and his crown to her courage and quick wit.

Beloved Samaritan

IT was the most tragic day in Walsall's long history of
disasters when a blast furnace exploded at the premises of
Jones & Son in Green Lane on the 15th of October in 1875.
A shower of red hot ashes and molten metal cascaded down
upon the nearest group of helpless workmen, inflicting appalling
injuries on all 14 of them. A gasp of petrified silence followed
the echo of the blast, then pandemonium reigned. Those fleeing
from the danger halted in their tracks and spun round aghast.
The two business partners in the nearby works office fearfully
raised their heads from the floor where they had swiftly ducked
for cover from flying cinders. The sight and sounds were
piteous. Then came a frantic call for somebody, somewhere,
to do something – to get to grips with the terrifying
consequences. All of the charred, almost unrecognisable human
forms still lived and breathed and were suffering unimaginable
pain and terror. Three of them somehow tottered into the canal
which flowed alongside. A workmate floundered in after them,
but felt utterly powerless to help.

The burden of responsibility in any crisis is crushing, and
Kenyon Jones, one of the two brothers who owned the works,
must have been beside himself with anguish. Hastily he thrust
off a messenger to the cottage hospital. It was already full, but
emergency plans went into immediate action. Blankets, linen
and improvised beds were called for and rapidly assembled while
the Sister in charge sped round to the works to give first aid
and superintend the lifting and transporting of the pitiful
casualties. The relief at Sister Dora's appearing, and of being
able to hand over to the cool-headed efficient nurse must have

117

been immense. She had coped with many emergencies in Walsall over the past ten years and her very presence inspired confidence and hope. Somehow the pitiful victims were conveyed through the streets to the big house called The Mount which had been converted from a girls' school into the local hospital. Once again its value as a refuge in frightful disaster, with Sister Dora in charge, was to prove inestimable.

Doctors were hastily summoned as the casualties were laid upon temporary cots but it became obvious that they saw little hope, if any, for the victims. In the days that followed surgeons and doctors were overcome with nausea at the daunting task and the foulness of the atmosphere, stumbling thankfully outdoors when their spell of duty was over. Yet the compassionate, resolute Sister stayed beside the patients day and night, treating, soothing, comforting and, when practical resources failed, breathing into their last hours something of her own strong spiritual resources and Christian faith. Within ten traumatic days the flicker of life left all but two of the men. 'Her strength is superhuman. I never saw such a woman,' ejaculated one of the doctors.

As well he might, for her achievements were phenomenal, despite her late start on the medical front. Hers was a remarkable story. When reaching her 20s in a Yorkshire rectory Dora (then Dorothy Pattison) had longed to join Florence Nightingale in the Crimea. But her way was resolutely blocked by a tyrannical clergyman father. In his eyes nursing was degrading, far below the dignity of any one of his eight daughters. Class distinction was very pronounced in the 19th century. Nursing hitherto had been in the hands of 'Mrs Gamp' types – half-drunken harridans with little or no medical knowledge, summoned in emergencies as midwives or as 'layers out'. Nursing was not recognized as a profession; this youngest daughter knew little of what she might face.

But family life in the rector's own home was worse even than that of the Barretts of Wimpole Street. Only the two sons had been allowed to leave home for school and university, and thus to escape the worst of their father's violent rages which bordered on mania and sometimes heralded a breakdown. Then the rector's inhuman treatment of their mother in her pitiful terminal illness arrested attempts by her daughters to flee the nest until death had released her.

Dorothy was over 30 (though always to look ten years younger than her age) before she made her stealthy bid for freedom by securing a teaching appointment with a tied cottage – and was almost lost to the nursing profession for ever. But in the following year the way opened to enrol in the Sisterhood of the Good Samaritans in the name of Sister Dora, and her life took on new meaning and direction. Despite the terrible past with her parson father, she regained her personal Christian faith and believed nursing was her calling, to serve sufferers as if she were serving Christ.

The training was rigorous with no scope whatever for initiative, but she was sent with an experienced nurse to a medical emergency in Walsall. Here a brilliance which would later become legendary began to emerge, together with a charm and diplomacy which made the people of Walsall take her to their hearts. During an epidemic of smallpox she was thrust in charge of the small cottage hospital then in Bridge Street and coped superbly with in-patients as well as those isolated in their homes. Walsall was a hive of industrial activity. Dangerous conditions produced the inevitable toll of accidents. Then, urged on by a doctor who recognised her genius, Sister Dora somehow found time to study ophthalmology, anatomy and dentistry. She was able to extract teeth and to perform minor but skilful operations unsupervised.

On surgery days it became recognised procedure that after superintending all routine preparations, she herself 'scrubbed up' and took her place at the table to act as house surgeon. Her strong hands worked deftly alongside the surgeon's. Perhaps more daring still in those days of protocol and male chauvinism, was her plucky intervention in persuading surgeons to consider alternatives before deciding too readily to perform amputations which might possibly be avoided.

A story which endeared Sister Dora to working folk sprang

from the experience of a badly injured workman whose right arm she saved by pleading with the surgeon to withhold amputation. 'Let me try . . .' was her plea. Within three weeks she saved the arm. It is related that the grateful patient afterwards spent many a Sunday striding the eleven miles to the hospital to pull the bell rope at the entrance with that precious arm, and to leave a glad message. 'Just tell her,' he would say with a confident smile, 'that her arm rang the bell.'

As the hectic years went on, Dora became more and more a part of Walsall's life, and grateful railmen presented her with a pony and trap for outside journeys. In 1872, the Pelsall Colliery disaster wrung the hearts of the whole town when the mine was suddenly flooded and 22 colliers were cut off from every possible escape route. For five days their families and officials at the pit head agonized as signals grew fainter and men died of exposure before a way of reaching them could be devised. Preparations to receive them at the hospital proved all in vain, so Sister Dora went out to bereaved homes and families to help them through the tragedy.

And now, three years later she was at the centre of the blast furnace tragedy. Throughout those epic ten days when the Sister refused to leave the sufferers, the works boss, Kenyon Jones, looked on and marvelled at the 44 year old nurse who coped night and day with scarcely an hour's respite – and the 29 year old businessman fell in love with her.

How strange a place for romance to blossom! And yet – where better? More revealing, perhaps, than weeks and months of 'normal' courtship! As for the age gap of 15 years between the two – this was of no consequence whatever to the tall, handsome, virile young man who saw the Sister as resourceful, energetic, a surprisingly youthful personality with a warm heart.

In view of the almost saint-like tributes to this extraordinary nurse, and superstitious legends springing up, even in her life time, that she possessed superhuman healing powers, it comes almost as a surprise to learn of her humanity. But one patient has left a spontaneous testimony to it. 'Laugh? She'd make you laugh if you were dying!' Maybe it was that blessed factor which stemmed the tide of advancing years and denied Father Time his victory in her life. Every evening at supper, however exhausting the day, she would regale her nurses with lively tales and spontaneous humour, giving them her whole attention except when emergency calls took priority. She left the supper table with a distinct void.

Small wonder, then, that Kenyon Jones fell under the spell of this slim, still attractive woman. Hitherto she had resolutely put her vocation before marriage, though once confessing that she would have loved children of her own. But she had long accepted that the hospital was her home; the patients her children. Yet now, as Kenyon Jones came week after week with fruit and other comforts for sick workers, and betrayed his feelings for her, Dora found an emotional response quickening in her own heart that went well beyond mere appreciation on her patients' behalf. She was tempted, and apparently yielded for more than a year to the luxury of loving and of being loved.

For some time the attachment, such as it was, was confined to happy co-operation in the wards. She and Kenyon together cheered the patients, and he put his ingenuity to work, devising various aids and equipment to better the lot of nurses and patients. It resulted in a little good-natured banter from the latter. Apart from this, it was very much a personal and private matter, with only occasional meetings away from the hospital. Kenyon attended church services in Wednesbury and Walsall when he knew Dora would be there, and other events provided meetings without drawing undue attention. While there was doubt as to what, if any, the outcome could be, it was unwise to meet openly. Perhaps the secrecy added some subtle appeal for them both. They exchanged letters (sometimes only brief notes). Fifty years on, some of Dora's letters to Kenyon came to light during a property clearance. Only then was this tender, secret interlude in Sister Dora's life revealed.

Sadly, it was not destined to be a happy-ever-after romance. Dora herself was conscious of the difference in age, and sensed a measure of reserve on the part of Kenyon's parents when visiting the home in Dudley. Marriage was incompatible with a woman's career then, especially so demanding a one as that which Dora had imposed upon herself. And, of course, anything less than marriage would not only violate her scruples but compromise her, undermining the trust she had inspired throughout these epic years. A nurse was not even supposed to receive a male visitor inside her office unchaperoned!

Dora was in a dilemma and felt the attachment had to end when there was danger of gossip, perhaps even of scandal, so she faced the challenge and made the break when Kenyon was called away for several months to South Africa. The few who knew of the liaison, or suspected it and feared for Dora's career, breathed again. Walsall could not spare her!

Or so it seemed. In this unpredictable world no one is indispensable. Shortly after the break with Kenyon came a devastating diagnosis for Dora from a private consultant outside her own hospital. Her own suspicions were confirmed; she was stricken with terminal cancer. For almost a year she concealed the news even from hospital colleagues, typically continuing to cast over her world the same aura of confidence and radiance which had characterized her brilliant 14 years of pioneering nursing in Walsall. At the end of that year, 1877, she gave a Christmas party, a reunion with former nurses, patients and children, which was a huge success. Not a shadow of suspicion crossed the minds of those present of what hung over her. When Kenyon returned from South Africa it seems that he had accepted the break and made no move. She feared him knowing her situation lest pity should drive him back when she could not resist.

1878 was to be a historic year in Walsall. A new hospital, largely designed and equipped by Dora, was on schedule and she was kept busy overseeing progress and equipping it with all the latest instruments she could lay hands upon. She was determined to live life to the full while she could. Then in March she had a surprise encounter with Kenyon Jones at a concert. Within hours the secret love was rekindled in them both. Despite her qualms and knowing Kenyon must soon discover her illness, the renewal gave her much joy.

A delay in the hospital building programme and signs of fatigue noticed by an unsuspecting senior consultant, resulted in her being despatched on a holiday pending the opening of the new hospital. She visited Yokshire, London and Paris (her first trip abroad) but on returning at the end of September she suffered a massive haemorrhage. Her secret was out.

There was no recourse now but to accept the little cottage on the Wednesbury road near the hospital gates chosen by the stunned and grieving medical board who gave her two weeks to live. Each evening Kenyon Jones was at her bedside and she surprised the doctors by having a period of remission. But when she neared the end of her extraordinary life and after an evening when her nurses had to turn him away because of her worsening condition Dora decided it was time to make the parting to save him further strain. Painfully, and with much heartache she penned a loving farewell, concluding:

> 'My darling I shall not see you again for it agitates me so much I feel almost it might kill me . . .
> Oh, Kenyon, you must not fret for me or grieve. I think I shall soon lay down the cross and I trust exchange it for a crown.
> Yours very faithfully, Sister Dora.'

Life did not flicker from her wasted form until Christmas Eve and the whole town mourned on December 28th. Shops were closed, works halted and blinds drawn everywhere as her funeral cortege passed through the streets of Walsall. Thousands followed the hearse on foot – The Mayor and Corporation, a Member of Parliament, clergy from every denomination in Walsall, two bishops, magistrates, schoolchildren and representatives from all walks of life. Railwaymen who had once provided her with a pony and carriage now felt honoured to bear her on their own shoulders for this last journey.

Citizens vied with each other in devising suitable memorials – naming the new hospital after her, a Memorial Convalescent

Home, a beautiful Sanctuary Window in St Matthew's Church, continuing her annual seaside holiday for patients and children, and erecting a beautiful full size bronze statue in the centre of the town. Among many tributes she was called 'a Princess of nurses', a Guardian Angel, a true Samaritan, and (what she would have liked best) lovingly claimed by the workpeople as Walsall's own Sister Dora.

Bibliography

The Leviathan of Wealth; The Sutherland Fortune in the Industrial Revolution by Eric Richards
Memoirs of the Dowager Lady Hardinge of Penshurst
King of Fools by John Parker
Sister Dora; The Life of Dorothy Pattison by Jo Manton
The Life of Sir Arthur Conan Doyle by John Dickson Carr
Murder and Mystery in the Black Country by Harold Parsons
Fragments of Stafford's Past by Dudley Wilkes
Folk Customs of Britain David MacFadyen and Christine Hole
Staffordshire by Arthur Mee in the King's England series
Reliques of English Poetry by Bishop T. Percy
Historic Staffordshire by Robert K. Dent and Joseph Hill, published by E.P. Publishing Ltd. (1975)
Urban and Industrial Songs of the Black Country and Birmingham by Jon Raven